# NATHAN THE WISE

By
PAUL D'ANDREA

after

G. E. LESSING

**Dramatic Publishing**
Woodstock, Illinois • England • Australia • New Zealand

For my brother,
Mark M. D'Andrea Jr.

# IMPORTANT BILLING AND CREDIT REQUIREMENTS

All producers of the Play *must* give credit to the Author(s) of the Play in all programs distributed in connection with performances of the Play and in all instances in which the title of the Play appears for purposes of advertising, publicizing or otherwise exploiting the Play and/or a production. The name of the author(s) *must* also appear on a separate line, on which no other name appears, immediately following the title, and *must* appear in size of type not less than fifty percent the size of the title type. Biographical information on the author(s), if included in the playbook, may be used in all programs. *In all programs this notice must appear:*

Produced by special arrangement with
THE DRAMATIC PUBLISHING COMPANY of Woodstock, Illinois

All producers of NATHAN THE WISE must include the following acknowledgment on the title page of all programs distributed in connection with performances of the play and on all advertising and promotional materials:

"Premiered by Theater of the First Amendment,
Fairfax, Virginia, on October 24, 2001.
Subsequently produced by Centro Dionysia, Rome, Italy,
on December 1, 2003."

NATHAN THE WISE was originally produced by Theater of the First Amendment (Rick Davis, Artistic Director, Kevin Murray, Managing Director and Kristin Johnsen-Neshati, Artistic Associate) in Fairfax, Virginia, in October 2001. It was directed by Tom Prewitt; translation by Gisela D'Andrea and Paul D'Andrea; set design by Anne Gibson; lighting design by Lisa L. Ogonowski; sound design by David McKeever; costume design by Jelena Vukmirovic; the technical director was Ethan Osborne; the dramaturg was Mary Resing; the company manager was Kira Hoffmann; the assistant scenic designer and property manager was Eileen Daly; and the production stage manager was Cary Louise Duschl. The cast was as follows:

Nathan ............................ MITCHELL HEBERT
Muslim Robber .................... CARLOS J. GONZALEZ
Christian Robber........................... KYLE PRUE
Saladin ........................... CRAIG WALLACE
Sittah........................... KIMBERLY SCHRAF
Heraklios............................ RALPH COSHAM
Curd von Stauffen......................... KYLE PRUE
Recha............................... MAIA DESANTI
Daya .............................. LYNNIE RAYBUCK
Bonfilio........................... MORGAN DUNCAN
Al-Hafi.......................... CARLOS J. GONZALEZ
Ensemble ..... BILLY CHACE, JEFF HINDMAN, JASON ROBERTS,
                PAUL SHERIDAN, NATHAN WOOLWINE

NATHAN THE WISE was produced by Il Centro Dionysia (Maria Nicoletta Gaida, Artistic Director) in Rome, Italy, in December 2003. It was directed by Domenico Polidoro, assisted by Andrea Baracco; the translation into Italian was by Georgia Gaida; with set design by Marco Brunetti; lighting design by Jurai Saleri; choreography by Francesco Manetti; original music by Massimo Torrefranca; costume design by Silvia Palmerani; the technical director was Enzo Ivan Sorbera; and the production stage manager was Anna Baldini. The cast was as follows:

Nathan ........................ ROBERTO MANTOVANI

Saladin . . . . . . . . . . . . . . . . . . . . . . . . . . . . . . ANTONIO TINTIS
Sittah . . . . . . . . . . . . . . . . . . . . . . . . GABRIELA TOMASSETTI
Heraklios . . . . . . . . . . . . . . . . RAFAELE MORELLATO LAMPIS
Curd von Stauffen . . . . . . . . . . . . . . . . . SANDRO CAMPAGNA
Recha . . . . . . . . . . . . . . . . . . . . . . . . . . . BEATRICE PRESEN
Daya . . . . . . . . . . . . . . . . . . . . . . . . . . . . . . . LUISA RICCI
Bonfilio . . . . . . . . . . . . . . . . . . . . . . . . FRANCESCO MANETTI
Al-Hafi . . . . . . . . . . . . . . . . . . . RAFAELE MORELLATO LAMPIS
Young Man/Angel . . . . . . . . . . . . . . . . . . . . ANDREA CAPALDI

NATHAN THE WISE was produced as a concert reading by
Theater of the First Amendment (Rick Davis, Artistic Director,
Kevin Murray, Managing Director and Kristin Johnsen-Neshati,
Artistic Associate) in Fairfax, Virginia, on September 11, 2004.
It was directed by Tom Prewitt; with set design by Anne Gibson; lighting design by Lisa L. Ogonowski; sound design by David McKeever; the technical director was Ethan Osborne; the
company manager was Kira Hoffmann; and the stage manager
was Lauren T. Hyland. The cast was as follows:

Nathan . . . . . . . . . . . . . . . . . . . . . . . . . F. MURRAY ABRAHAM
Muslim Robber . . . . . . . . . . . . . . . . . . . . CARLOS J. GONZALEZ
Christian Robber . . . . . . . . . . . . . . . . . . . . . . . PAUL TAKACS
Saladin . . . . . . . . . . . . . . . . . . . . . . . . . . . CRAIG WALLACE
Sittah . . . . . . . . . . . . . . . . . . . . . . . . . . . KIMBERLY SCHRAF
Heraklios . . . . . . . . . . . . . . . . . . . . . . . . . . . RALPH COSHAM
Curd von Stauffen . . . . . . . . . . . . . . . . . . . . . PAUL TAKACS
Recha . . . . . . . . . . . . . . . . . . . . . . . . . . COLLEEN DELANEY
Daya . . . . . . . . . . . . . . . . . . . . . . . . . . ROSEMARY KNOWER
Bonfilio . . . . . . . . . . . . . . . . . . . . . . . . . . MORGAN DUNCAN
Al-Hafi . . . . . . . . . . . . . . . . . . . . . . . . CARLOS J. GONZALEZ

NATHAN was produced for PBS broadcast by WETA/TV in
Washington, D.C., in January 2002 with the original cast. The
producer was Jackson Frost; the director was Joseph Camp; the
executive producer was Jim Corbley; the executive in charge
was Dalton Delan.

# AUTHOR'S NOTES

At the beginning of the play Nathan speaks the first four verses of the Twenty-Third Psalm in Hebrew and then breaks off as he begins the fifth. "The Lord is my shepherd; I shall not want...Thou preparest a table before me..."

The script provides a phonetic rendering of the Hebrew words. The letters "ch" are pronounced as in "Johann Sebastian Bach."

The displays of skill with sword and scimitar in I.5 can be replaced with a choreographed duel, perhaps with dervish circlings for Saladin.

PRONUNCIATION

| | |
|---|---|
| Al-Hafi | ahl hah FEE |
| Assad | ah SAHD |
| Ayyubites | AYE you bites |
| Bonfilio | bawn FEEL lee o |
| Darun | dah ROON |
| Daya | DIE uh |
| Heraklios | hair AHK lee us |
| Recha | RAY kuh |
| Saladin | sahl uh DEEN |
| Shariah | SHA ree ah |
| Siloa | sill OH uh |
| Sittah | SEE tah |
| von Stauffen | vawn SHTAU fin |
| Wolf von Filnek | WOLF vawn FILL neck |

This play is an adaptation of Gotthold Ephraim Lessing's *Nathan the Wise*. Lessing wrote *Nathan* in 1779 in honor of his friend Moses Mendelssohn, the advocate of Jewish emancipation, civil rights and enlightenment.

*Nathan* also presents a compelling portrait of Saladin, the Islamic warrior sultan, the George Washington of Muslim history. The story is based on the 1192 battle among Christian, Jew and Muslim for control of Jerusalem. The resolution comes from a challenge based on the concept of "the People of the Book," the surprising commonality of the three monotheistic faiths.

The challenge is itself based on ideas from Boccaccio's 1352 "Parable of the Rings" (*Decameron*, I.3).

# NATHAN THE WISE

A Play in Two Acts
For 6 Men and 3 Women

CHARACTERS
(in order of appearance)

NATHAN . . . . . . . . . . . . . . a wise and wealthy Jew, 60s
MUSLIM ROBBER (doubled by Al-Hafi)
CHRISTIAN ROBBER (doubled by Curd)
SALADIN . . . the sultan of the Middle East from Egypt to
Syria, ruling in Jerusalem, 55
SITTAH . . . . . . . . . . . . . . . . . . Saladin's sister, late 40s
HERAKLIOS . . . . . . . . . Christian Patriarch of Jerusalem
RECHA . . . . . . . . . . . . . . . . . . . . Nathan's daughter, 16
DAYA . . . . . . . . . . . . . . . . . . . . Recha's governess, 40s
EXECUTED TEMPLARS (doubled by Sittah and Nathan)
EXECUTIONER (doubled by Al-Hafi)
CURD VON STAUFFEN . . a Christian Knight Templar, 24
BONFILIO . . . . . . . . . . . . . . . . . . . . . . . . . a friar, 50s
AL-HAFI . . a Muslim whirling dervish, a mendicant monk,
40s

TIME AND SETTING:
The year is 1192. The place: Jerusalem at the time of the
Third Crusade (1189-1192), during a truce offered by
Saladin, victorious leader of the Saracens against the Cru-
saders.

# ACT I

## SCENE 1

*(Although we can't see him yet, we hear NATHAN praying, wailing like a cantor, as he walks alongside his caravan in the desert. He is singing the 23rd Psalm.)*

NATHAN *(off)*. Ha-SHEM RO-EE. LOH ech-SAR. Bin-OHT DE-SHEH yar-bi-TSAY-nee.

*(NATHAN enters. He has been traveling for more than six months, and is now about twenty miles from Jerusalem. Although he is strong, the journey has taken its toll on his almost seventy-year-old body. He climbs a rise, and looks out. In the distance he can see Jerusalem gleaming.)*

NATHAN *(cont'd)*. Al-MAY me-noo-CHOT ye-nah ha-LAY-nee. Naph-SHEE ye-sho-VEV yan-CHE-nee ve-mah-geh-LAYEE TSE-dek le-MA-an she-MOH. *(Raising his hands to the heavens.)* GAM kee ay-LECH be-GAYEE tsal-MA-vet, loh-EE-RAH RAH kee-ah-TAH ee-mah-DEE shiv-te-CHA—

*(Unseen by NATHAN, two men—a MUSLIM ROBBER and a CHRISTIAN ROBBER—approach him stealthily.)*

NATHAN *(cont'd).* —oo-mish-an-TE-cha HAY-mah
ye-nah-cha-MOO-nee. TAH-ah-ROCH—

*(CROSS-FADE TO:)*


## SCENE 2

*(SALADIN, the sultan, strides to a public platform and
stands between his sister SITTAH and the Christian
Patriarch HERAKLIOS. CROWD noises.)*

SALADIN. I, Saladin, Improver of the World, have just re-
turned from viewing the devastation of war. In disguise,
I walked among the people. I saw old men and women
crying, their leather faces so wrinkled the tears couldn't
flow, caught in the creases like streams on a mountain. I
saw a woman with dead eyes lullaby a dying child. I
questioned: Why don't they revive the babe, husband the
wife and bring harvest home? I therefore declare there
shall be a truce in Jerusalem. *(SITTAH and HERAKLIOS
are shocked.)* The treasure hitherto consumed by war
shall be given to the poor. Christian and Jew may live in
peace with Muslims. *(The CROWD breaks into shouts of
joy and cries of "Truce in Jerusalem!" "O mighty
Saladin!" and "Peace in our time!")* Death to the man
who breaks my law.

*(Angry, SITTAH turns and strides off. SALADIN follows
her with his eyes and then turns to look at HERAKLIOS,
who serenely brings his hands together in prayer.
CROSS-FADE TO:)*

## SCENE 3

*(NATHAN is kneeling by his campfire. The TWO MEN approach NATHAN from behind. One has a broken piece of wood in his hand. The other has a knife. Without moving and without looking at them, NATHAN speaks.)*

NATHAN. I'm baking bread. Can you smell it? It's pretty good. Considering there's no leaven. But, you know, any bread's good when you're hungry. *(The TWO MEN stop.)* In a few minutes it's ready. Eat with me. My caravan's rich. Richer, friends, than you can possibly rob. Eat. Put on new clothes. I'll give you more than you can steal—and we'll walk together the last day's journey to holy Jerusalem. See? There. *(NATHAN points to Jerusalem, out in the distance.)* Look, out there! The turrets of Jerusalem. The Dome of the Rock. The Tower of David. The Mount of Olives. The madness and the hope of all mankind meet, there—see!—there, in the dreaming city of Jerusalem. And, look! The setting sun has like a hunter cast a lariat around the turrets of Saladin, and edged them in gold. *(NATHAN turns to the TWO MEN.)* You are Christian and Muslim.

CHRISTIAN ROBBER. You are Nathan.

NATHAN. I am. Join a Jew in prayer.

MUSLIM ROBBER. To whom?

NATHAN. The one God.

CHRISTIAN ROBBER. You're a rabbi.

NATHAN. No, I'm not.

MUSLIM ROBBER. They call you Nathan the Wise.

NATHAN. I remember what I've seen and I have a pretty good idea of what I don't know. Is that wise, or is that common sense? Come.

CHRISTIAN ROBBER. Those Hebrew words. What do they mean?

NATHAN. "Thou preparest a table before me, in the presence of mine enemies. Thou anointest my head with oil, my cup runneth over."

CHRISTIAN ROBBER. Ah. *(He kneels and crosses himself.)* "Surely goodness and mercy shall follow me all the days of my life."

*(The MUSLIM ROBBER kneels and prostrates himself.)*

MUSLIM ROBBER. "And I will dwell in the house of the Lord for ever."

*(NATHAN offers his bread to the TWO MEN. They tear off pieces of the bread.)*

CHRISTIAN ROBBER. Why do you help us?

NATHAN. I'm a man. I consider nothing that is human to be alien to me.

MUSLIM ROBBER. You give us bread. What do you want?

NATHAN. A husband for my daughter.

MUSLIM ROBBER. Hah!

NATHAN. Don't worry. I didn't have you in mind.

MUSLIM ROBBER. I meant—so rich and so foolish.

CHRISTIAN ROBBER. Nathan. We'll eat your bread.

MUSLIM ROBBER. But we won't take your money.

*(The TWO MEN start to exit.)*

CHRISTIAN ROBBER. May I say, Nathan. With this piece of bread and with peace in our time, we could earn our own money.

MUSLIM ROBBER. And so. Aspire higher, rabbi.

*(NATHAN looks at them in surprise. The TWO MEN exit. CROSS-FADE TO:)*

## SCENE 4

*(In NATHAN's house. RECHA and DAYA.)*

RECHA. Oh, no, good nurse Daya. No one will ever take the place of my father Nathan! I have the best there ever was.

DAYA. That's what all the foolish young girls say. But now you are a woman! And now there is a truce. You can marry. I tell you, Recha, find a handsome young prince and run off with him. Perhaps to France. That way you can be a Christian! Like me! And then I can get back to France! To my home in Anjou. To Anjou, my poupou!

RECHA. I'm not your poupou. And I don't want to go to Anjou. I'm the daughter of a virtuous Jew. Why should I become a Christian?

DAYA. Aha!

RECHA. You're always aha-ing.

DAYA. If I could only talk!

RECHA. And there's another! What does that mean?

DAYA. I must not speak. I must be forever silent, tassle-turn, and even thumbstruck. But you, Recha, should long to be in love! Ah! Love! Love! Love!

RECHA. If love, love, love is so wonderful, why do you reject Al-Hafi? He's loved you ardent and faithful all these years!

DAYA. Al-Hafi is not a Christian. He is most irreligious. A Muslim. A disbeliever. An infantile! Perhaps even a Hereford! But if you fell in love with a Christian, then my most ardent wish would be fulfilled. To see you back in Europe, among people worthy of you.

RECHA. You love your people and I love you for it. But I want to stay with my father Nathan.

DAYA. Aha! Nathan!

RECHA. Yes, Nathan! What did he ever do to you, that you always try to seek my happiness elsewhere, away from him?

DAYA (darkly). If I could only talk.

RECHA. Daya, my darling, you talk all the time.

DAYA. Is your life perfect?

RECHA. Yes! It is, so leave it alone. It will be, if my father gets back safe to me. No, it isn't. Look at these wars! Daya, what if in this truce—Moses and Jesus and Muhammad appeared and told us to stop the wars! What if the three of them just showed up one fine day, arm in arm! Then the world would listen!

DAYA. Stop your fantasies! I know what's best for you. Fall in love. With some fine young man gleaming like an angel.

RECHA (smiling in spite of herself). An angel! Oh, Daya! A typical excellent, practical plan! And my dear nurse, how will I know that I've met a man like an angel?

DAYA. You'll know.
RECHA. How?
DAYA. Your knees will go weak.


## SCENE 5

*(SALADIN enters. He's angry. As he speaks, he's half dragging, half throwing about FIRST KNIGHT TEMPLAR.)*

SALADIN *(enraged)*. Blood, you see, blood, flowed over my ankles on the battlefield! And in a ditch I saw a woman with dead eyes lullabying a child. *(SALADIN seizes a SECOND KNIGHT TEMPLAR, and throws him about.)* I—am—the—sultan. Improver of the world. But my title was a mockery in my throat. So I made a truce!

*(SALADIN has set up the two KNIGHTS TEMPLAR for execution. The EXECUTIONER enters, leading another Templar, CURD VON STAUFFEN.)*

SALADIN *(cont'd)*. You Knights Templar are mortal ene-mies of the Muslim faith. I let you live. And then you broke the truce! *(Beat.)* Execute them all. *(The FIRST and SECOND TEMPLARS bow their heads. The EXE-CUTIONER lifts his sword.)* You, leader of the Templars. Why did you break the truce?
CURD. My life had become a hollow nut.
SALADIN. What did you expect?
CURD. To die.
SALADIN. What do you expect?

CURD. Death.

*(CURD turns. SALADIN stares at him and is surprised at what he sees.)*

SALADIN. Serve me.
CURD. Impossible. I'm dead.
SALADIN. Then you're free of obligations. Serve me.
CURD. I will serve only a soldier better than myself.
SALADIN. Your rash statement convinces me. *(To the EX-ECUTIONER.)* Give this man your sword. *(The EXECU-TIONER gives CURD the sword. To CURD:)* Show me your skill.

*(CURD takes the sword, raises it over his head, and brings it crashing down on a wooden beam. He cuts the beam in two. SALADIN draws a piece of silk from his clothing. He throws it in the air. He draws his scimitar, and before the silk can fall, SALADIN cuts it into many pieces with his rapidly flashing scimitar. SALADIN points with his scimitar to the beam and the silk.)*

SALADIN *(cont'd)*. Templar. Saladin. *(CURD kneels and presents the sword to SALADIN.)*
CURD. You are the greater warrior. My life is yours.
SALADIN *(to his SOLDIERS)*. Spare his life.
EXECUTIONER. Why, O Saladin?

*(SALADIN fixes the EXECUTIONER with a look.)*

SALADIN. Because once, a long time ago, my brother Assad was lost. He was a jewel of great price. A sun-filled opal that I loved. Do it because once a babe was burnt and naked. Do it because it is the will of Saladin. *(To CURD.)* You have the freedom of the city. Do not leave Jerusalem. I have your word?

CURD. Yes.

SALADIN. Come to me tomorrow.

CURD. I shall.

EXECUTIONER. And the others?

SALADIN. Why, you'll have to kill them, won't you?

*(Exit SALADIN. CURD recovers his poise, straightens, and swirls his cape. We can see that it is white with a red cross. He walks off. We see the sword being raised and then LIGHTS OUT.)*

## SCENE 6

*(FRIAR BONFILIO is in attendance upon the Christian Patriarch HERAKLIOS. BONFILIO has an obsessive hand-wringing gesture that makes him look servile.)*

HERAKLIOS. Saladin is a severe observer of the law. Yet. The truce has been broken. And a Templar was spared by Saladin, who executed all the other truce-breakers. Find out why. *(HERAKLIOS hands a letter to BON-FILIO.)* Bear my message, just as I gave it to you, to the— *(enjoying the word)* Christian—Templar.

BONFILIO. O Heraklios, I cannot!

HERAKLIOS. *Just* as I gave it to you, on pain of excommunication.

BONFILIO. Yes, Eminence.

HERAKLIOS. Then find out everything you can about the Jew, Nathan.

BONFILIO. Yes, Patriarch.

HERAKLIOS. The wealth of the caravan. How he got his money.

BONFILIO. Through trade.

HERAKLIOS. Yes, trade, but sometimes there are little dubieties, little hedges. Saladin worships the law. Find out where Nathan has broken the law. Everyone breaks the law. Oh. And see if this Nathan has made any seditious remarks against Saladin. Maybe a jest, in wine. When you give confession, has anyone—?

BONFILIO. Master, I'll die on the rack before I'll reveal a syllable of any confession I have heard.

HERAKLIOS. Of course. So would I. You know this Nathan has publicly refused me money.

BONFILIO. He gives direct to the poor. Of all religions.

HERAKLIOS. Yes. He's very well liked, isn't he.

BONFILIO. Jews are free to live in Jerusalem. Free to be liked.

HERAKLIOS. Under the law. Don't forget the law. *(Beat.)* Friar. Come over here. Come here. *(BONFILIO obeys.)* Jesus never touched me.

BONFILIO. Master?

HERAKLIOS. I never had any of His blood. Those bleeding hands. The wound in His side. He has never appeared to me, nor has He dictated to me as Gabriel did to Muhammad. I've never seen dried red blood crusted on braided damask. And so I rely on law and dogma. Don't you see? Since I'm not sure, I must therefore be certain. So I wage war to win. I do what I do because Jesus never touched me with His eloquent blood.

BONFILIO. Give me your blessing.

*(HERAKLIOS blesses BONFILIO, and they exit separate ways.)*


## SCENE 7

*(SALADIN and his sister, SITTAH, are playing chess in the palace of SALADIN.)*

SITTAH. I told you to kill them all!

*(SITTAH slams a chess piece. SALADIN slams a chess piece.)*

SALADIN. I killed them!
SITTAH *(slams a chess piece)*. You freed the leader!
SALADIN *(slams a chess piece)*. Allah is merciful.

*(The following is a blitz of quick chess moves from both players, as if the cities being mentioned were right on the board.)*

SITTAH. You conquered Jerusalem. You conquered Egypt. You don't have Akka! You conquered Damascus, Sidon, Tyre, Caesarea, Joppa. But you don't have the port of Akka! As long as the Templars have Akka, they repair their wounds and come at you again. You must have money to conquer Akka! You fight a hundred-headed hydra, until you have Akka. Your truce stopped you from having Akka. And then they broke the truce! You don't have money. You don't have peace. And you don't have Akka.

SALADIN. Akka! Akka! The truth is, sister, at your age of the moon, the blood does not flow—

SITTAH. That's right, Saladin! It doesn't! It does not! And so I hunger for blood. If our family line dies out, I want blood and I want money. *(SITTAH moves a chess piece.)* You need money.

SALADIN. All I need is one coat. One horse. One sword. One God. *(SALADIN moves a piece.)*

SITTAH. One faith! *(SITTAH slams a piece.)*

SALADIN. One God. There's a difference.

SITTAH. Seize the wealth of Nathan the Jew.

SALADIN. Nathan lives safe under the law, which I enforce. Jews are People of the Book. They're welcome in a Jerusalem governed by Saladin.

SITTAH. The Christians are defeated. The Jews have no power. Now is the time. Seize his wealth. Imprison him.

SALADIN. You forget, my dear sister. I uphold the laws. So don't break them or I'll throw *you* in jail.

SITTAH. Nathan has more money than you do.

SALADIN *(smiling)*. Why shouldn't he? He's a much more able businessman. Besides, he exceeds the giving prescribed by Islam. By quite a bit.

SITTAH. In the time you're taking to make one move, I could personally ride out and take Akka.

SALADIN. My sword's in the hall.

SITTAH. The Christians won't stay defeated. Look at your truce. Christians attack. That's what they do, by unblinking instinct, unthinking. They want our country. Look around you. Are we in Europe? No. But they are here, in Arabia. *(SITTAH slams the chessboard with her hand.)*

Are we in Paris? No! But they occupied Jerusalem for eighty years until you drove them out, not with your reason's edge, brother, but with your scimitar's blade! *(Beat.)* And lost your son in doing it. *(SALADIN freezes.)* The last child of our line! *(SALADIN fights for control.)* I have none! And can have none! Our brother Assad is dead at Askalon! We are all that is left of the Ayyubites! Don't trust the Christians! They broke the truce once. They'll break it again. Their founder, Jesus, peace be upon him, is the Prince of Peace, and yet the Christians are the Kings of War!

SALADIN. A woman of your ferocity should have had Assad as your warrior Sultan. No truces with Assad! Off with their heads!

SITTAH. They slaughtered civilians, eighty years ago!

SALADIN. Allah is merciful, wise and compassionate.

SITTAH. That's Allah.

SALADIN. You're impious!

SITTAH. Be compassionate to your own people.

SALADIN. What if my people are all mankind?

SITTAH. You're mad! What! Indians and Mongolians? The blood of the Ayyubites. These are your people. The family of Islam.

SALADIN. I am Saladin. My joy is in the Koran.

SITTAH. And what does the holy Koran tell you?

SALADIN. To be the Improver of the World.

SITTAH. How better to improve it than to make Islam the One True Faith! We *know*— *(wiggling the chess piece as if she would drive it through the board)* we have the true religion. And so we should sweep away the infidel. Check. We possess the ring of the Ayyubites. We are certain. Check. Expel the Christians. Seize the wealth of Nathan.

SALADIN. Certainty is murder. You should kill a man sometime, Sittah. It would do wonders for your world view.

*(FRIAR BONFILIO enters. He continues his obsessive hand-wringing gesture.)*

BONFILIO *(bowing)*. Lady. Oh, Saladin! My master the Patriarch Heraklios sends me to tell you that he is coming at your request, to agree upon the laws that will govern the truce.

SALADIN. Thank you, good Friar. What is your name?

BONFILIO. Bonfilio.

SALADIN. Good Bonfilio, I'm just a man. Like you. There's no need for the hand-wringing. Deference, not servility.

BONFILIO. I know, Excellence. An arrow-tip lodged in the bone of my hand. I think that's why I do it. That would be my guess.

SALADIN. Where did this happen?

BONFILIO. At Askalon.

*(SALADIN and SITTAH look at each other.)*

SALADIN. Were you a warrior?

BONFILIO *(smiling; for a moment he's handsome)*. I was not always a priest. All honor to you and Lady Sittah. *(Exit BONFILIO.)*

SALADIN. There's more to that man than meets the eye. Strange that he should serve Heraklios.

SITTAH. I hate Heraklios! I hate him! Is it legal, in the Shariah, to hate a Patriarch?

SALADIN. Why should I answer? You'll pay no attention.

SITTAH. He destroyed my marriage to the English prince. A marriage that might have ended a war.

SALADIN. Did you love the prince?

SITTAH. Why do you ask?

SALADIN. I have my reasons. Did you love him?

SITTAH. I have no idea! I listened to his declarations with an icy spine. But I was in a passion to marry him. The alliance would have united crusader and Saracen. The port of Akka would have been my dowry.

SALADIN. But did you want the prince, peace or Akka?

SITTAH *(tips over the chessboard, screams)*. Akka! *(Contemptuously.)* Love! I laughed at that illusion right from the start! Heraklios demanded that I become Christian to marry the English prince. As if Christians alone had a claim on love! Our creator granted it to any man and woman!

*(Enter AL-HAFI.)*

AL-HAFI. Have they finally arrived? The monies out of Egypt? I hope there are mountains of monies. With foothills. So we can pay our debts! *(AL-HAFI sees the chess pieces on the floor.)* Religious war, devastation, and endemic poverty are one thing. But these are chess pieces! On the floor! Like pebbles! This ought not to be. This comes close to sacrilege. *(AL-HAFI studies the chess pieces.)* I see the game and the discussion were going badly for you, Saladin.

SALADIN. How do you know that?

AL-HAFI. The highly revealing positions of the chess
   pieces.

SALADIN *(peering at the pieces)*. What positions?

AL-HAFI. Knocked over. *(Beat.)* The caravan?

SALADIN. There's no caravan.

AL-HAFI. One day it will come as a great shock to your
   nervous system, O Saladin, when you realize that giving
   me the title "Treasurer of the Sultan" does not put any
   money in the coffers. We need money. Real money,
   preferably out of Egypt. You know? "Chink, chink." It
   comes in bags? I can't pay debts with a title. *(SALADIN
   fixes him with a stare.)* Oh, cut off my head if you will!
   Living in this pokey little town of Jerusalem I have no
   real need for it. But I bow out of this elaborate charade.
   You have no money. You are broke. Flat. Bust. Empty.
   Gone. Impoverished. Sitting in an empty space. Desti-
   tute, down-and-out. Saladin, you are badly off, indigent,
   penurious, ruined, wiped out, insolvent. Your resources
   financial are meager, scanty, skimpy, sparse, scarce, pal-
   try, slight, trivial. You have little cash. How can I say
   this? You're not good with money, O Saladin. *(Looking
   at the chess pieces.)* And on top of it all—the final in-
   sult—chess pieces! On the floor! Ripped from their in-
   cubating squares! *(SALADIN and SITTAH look at him.
   They don't get it.)* Where they hatch plots! Which you
   should do! To get money!

SALADIN. For me, one coat, one horse, one sword—

AL-HAFI. That's good, 'cause one of each is all you're
   ever going to have. You haven't got the cash for two.

SALADIN. Al-Hafi, I had counted on a surplus in your
   coffers.

AL-HAFI. *You* made me give away all your money. *(Mimicking SALADIN.)* "Improve the world. No one is to be poor." No one but you. I should have embezzled. At least there'd be some money! Oh, the injustice! That I, to whose magic fingers purses leap of their own accord— *(Suddenly worried, patting himself, searching for any purses he may have absentmindedly snatched.)* you *do* have all your possessions, don't you?— *(SALADIN is unconcerned.)* —that I should watch all the money in the treasury trickle away like water into sand.

SITTAH. There *is* a caravan. *(SALADIN looks at her in surprise.)* Not ours. *(To AL-HAFI.)* Your friend is back.

AL-HAFI *(stunned)*. Friend?

SITTAH. Your much-admired Jew.

AL-HAFI. Jew? Admired? By me? Much?

SITTAH. His caravan is just outside Jerusalem. To quote you: "He's the one man to whom God has given both wisdom and wealth."

AL-HAFI. I should have said that of a Jew? Me? To whom, dear lady, do you refer?

SITTAH. Nathan.

AL-HAFI. Oh! Nathan.

SITTAH. Nathan the Wise.

AL-HAFI. He's not my friend. Maybe we used to play a little chess.

SALADIN. He's rich?

AL-HAFI. In the old days, maybe. No more. Oh no, he's a goner. Lost it all in, uh, speculation. In…wheat, and, uh, mineral futures. I think. Yes.

SITTAH. My spies tell me Jerusalem will be in awe of the treasures he's brought sparkling back from India and Samarkand.

AL-HAFI. Oh. All right. So he's rich again. Maybe he's wise again.

SITTAH. Could you approach him?

*(AL-HAFI begins to spin and dance. By the time he's done he's spun himself right out of the room.)*

AL-HAFI. No. That's out of the question. He's wise because—uh—he doesn't lend.

SITTAH. That's not what you used to say.

AL-HAFI. He gives to the poor. Irrespective of religion. Jew, Christian, Muslim, Buddhist, Taoist, Hindu or Zoroastrian, it's all the same to him.

SALADIN. I will summon him.

AL-HAFI *(edging toward the door)*. But, it's all given away, don't you see. And besides, between ourselves, I'm not on the most cordial terms with him right now. No-siree. I must be going. I'll see what I can do to raise money elsewhere. Knock on other doors. Hear other voices. Work other rooms.

SITTAH. Useless rascal!

AL-HAFI. Oh. The friar told me Heraklios is on his way here. A word to the wise: the Patriarch is a great man, but he is a specialist in afterthoughts. Beware of his afterthoughts.

*(Exit AL-HAFI. He then appears upstage. LIGHTS DOWN off SALADIN as he is lost in thought. SITTAH crosses to soliloquize.)*

SITTAH. I will use Nathan's gold to besiege and win Akka. And then the one true faith will spread over all the world. Are we in Paris? No. But we will be.

*(As AL-HAFI soliloquizes, DAYA appears, with her broom. She watches him, unobserved. AL-HAFI begins to spin as he incants. As he does, DAYA, in spite of herself, slowly begins to twirl in imitation.)*

AL-HAFI.
>  To Nathan will I post
>  To circumvent an evil.
>  In Nathan's granary,
>  Will Sittah prove a weevil.
>  Heraklios not a priest,
>  He were then the devil.

*(LIGHTS DOWN off AL-HAFI. DAYA keeps spinning. She then stops, and shakes her head vigorously to get the nonsense out of it. She sweeps as if her life depended on it.)*

### SCENE 8

*(NATHAN is walking. He is now a few miles outside of Jerusalem.)*

NATHAN. Who's there!

*(AL-HAFI appears.)*

AL-HAFI. Go ahead. Stare at me, and take your time.

NATHAN. My old chess companion, Al-Hafi! *(They embrace.)* Is that really you?

AL-HAFI. None other.

NATHAN. How is my daughter Recha?

AL-HAFI. She's well.

NATHAN. Ahh!

AL-HAFI. And well cared for by her nurse, the beauteous Daya.

NATHAN. Still pursuing that forbidden fruit. I told you—forget about Daya. But Recha? Recha?

AL-HAFI. Six months older. Quite a young lady. As always, full of daring ideas. And, your Recha is a true beauty. She shines like a star in a corporeal veil.

NATHAN. Yes, she's pretty, isn't she? But I never let her know that, Al-Hafi. Oh, no. No, no, no, no. I am stern with her.

AL-HAFI. I've noticed. Very stern.

NATHAN. Yes. You know, when she goes off on her flights of imagination. I chastise her—

AL-HAFI. Very rigorously. It's actually terrifying.

NATHAN. Oh, yes. Truth is, her daring mind will one day take her far beyond me. Soon I'll be back with her. What joy! But, Al-Hafi! What are you doing in such a get-up?

AL-HAFI *(spinning to show it off)*. I am now Saladin's treasurer.

NATHAN. You, a dervish!

AL-HAFI. Dervishes have to get ahead just like everybody else.

NATHAN. Nonsense.

AL-HAFI. He persuaded me. He sweet-talked me into it.

NATHAN. Al-Hafi, you're a thief.

AL-HAFI. True.

NATHAN. No offense intended.

AL-HAFI. None taken.

NATHAN. I mean, by nature, you steal things. I haven't felt for my purse since we embraced, but I will bet you one contemplative camel, that my purse is tucked in the folds of your robe.

AL-HAFI *(handing NATHAN the purse)*. So it is. You're right. It's like breathing. I don't even think about it.

NATHAN. Thank you.

AL-HAFI. It's all there.

NATHAN. How did Saladin persuade you?

AL-HAFI. He said only a beggar knows how beggars feel. So he chose me to give money to beggars. He wants to make them all well-off! Saladin's goal is to live up to his title. "Improver of the World."

NATHAN. A noble goal.

AL-HAFI. No one is to be poor. No one in the world! How can he do that?

NATHAN. Not while fighting the crusaders.

AL-HAFI. Nathan. Saladin's a warrior, not a banker. He wants to do good, but money slips through his fingers like water scooped from the River Jordan. Lady Sittah knows of this rich caravan.

NATHAN. So—

AL-HAFI. So he will summon you. And borrow till you're poor, and all the little mice, all the little mousies, die down dead in your empty haylofts, that were never bare before.

NATHAN. I know my mind.

AL-HAFI. Nathan. Be careful of Saladin. Be cautious around ceaselessly strategic Sittah. But beware of the Christian Patriarch, Heraklios. Saladin is restrained by his veneration for the law. But Heraklios will use any tool to hand—

NATHAN. To hurt a Jew?

AL-HAFI. To hurt *you*. And take your wealth.

NATHAN. I hate to seem inquisitive, but do I have everything I came with?

AL-HAFI *(handing him a gold chain)*. Now you do.

NATHAN. You missed this. *((NATHAN reveals a purse made out of cloth of gold.)* Let me show you the priceless rings I found in Samarkand and Babylon.

AL-HAFI. No, the temptation would be too great. I must go. Salaam alaykum.

NATHAN. Shalom.


*(Exit AL-HAFI.)*


## SCENE 9


*(Night. Wind blowing. NATHAN is finally arriving in front of his house. Commotion. DAYA comes running toward NATHAN.)*


DAYA. Nathan! We're lost! Your house is on fire!

NATHAN. Where's Recha?

DAYA. Trapped! Inside!

NATHAN. Recha! Recha! We've got to get her out!

DAYA. It's a furnace! *(NATHAN runs toward the house.)* No! You'll burn!

*(CURD runs up, knocks NATHAN and DAYA aside and rushes into the burning house. SOUNDS of the house falling. CURD comes out of the house with RECHA in his arms.)*

NATHAN. My daughter! *(CURD gives RECHA's limp body to NATHAN and leaves, his white cape flying.)* What miracle is this?

RECHA. Father!

NATHAN. Yes, Recha. I'm right here.

DAYA. You were saved by an angel, with white wings!

NATHAN. Daya, stop that! Here! The garden house is safe! *(NATHAN carries RECHA to a couch, and gently sets her down. DAYA caresses RECHA's face.)*

DAYA. How close we were to ruin!

NATHAN. You were saved by a Christian knight.

DAYA. He was an angel!

NATHAN. No nonsense, Daya, please!

RECHA. Yes! I think I saw his wings!

DAYA. An angel.

NATHAN. Even more amazing—he was a Christian warrior knight. How can a Templar live in Jerusalem?

DAYA. Miraculously pardoned by Saladin. Today!

RECHA. I was saved by an angel sent by the sultan?

NATHAN *(caressing her face)*. No, no, my dear. That is just another hypothesis à la Daya.

DAYA. Mock on, Nathan. You will find you can't mock God.

NATHAN. I wasn't mocking God, my dear Daya, I was mocking you. One day you will realize there is a sizable difference. Daya, I must give thanks for this miracle.

DAYA. To the knight?

NATHAN *(jubilantly)*. To God! For this mitzvah, this blessing! "Rabbi, aspire higher!" *(To DAYA.)* Let her sleep. As soon as Recha wakes, seek out this Templar.

DAYA. He's an angel.

NATHAN. Well, in that case you'll probably find him hovering at low altitude. Just pull him down to you and hold on.

DAYA. If I could only talk!

NATHAN. No one's stopping you, Daya.

DAYA. If!

NATHAN. Hush. She sleeps. You'll wake her with your prattling ifs. Come, old menace! Withdraw.

DAYA. Oh, to be speechless! Condemned to be eternally mutable! I am the helpless prawn of fate!

*(NATHAN and DAYA exit. RECHA tosses and turns on the couch. She sits up.)*

RECHA. Can I love? Could I? This man? Who saved me? Let's not be giddy, Recha! But I think I could. Love him. He has a green eye and Hermes' curls. But manly, not a boy. A dimpled jaw, but manly. A powerful jaw, a jaw like Mount Zion, on which the temple stood. Arms like cedars. A fierce, penetrating eye. But one that could be kind. That could melt. Tears. For one he loved. A woman he loved. Were he to love. But, he is not perfect. Think of that, foolish Recha! He didn't stay. He's troubled.

*(DAYA appears, approaches, and remains unseen while she listens to RECHA.)*

RECHA *(cont'd)*. He's no Nathan. Ah! Nathan. What would Nathan think? Well, Recha, never mind your father. No. Hey, no. Never mind. This is an affair of the heart. *Une affaire de coeur. (A smile from DAYA.)* Fathers don't count in such things. Templars do. Time to spread one's amatory wings. Fly. Fly from the nest. This is no time for reason. Love and reason are not bedfellows. Whereas lovers are. The Templar is like a troubled stream, that doesn't know where to flow. No bed. Oh. I don't think I'm ready for this. Why should I fly from my nest? I like my nest.

*(DAYA comes forward.)*

RECHA *(cont'd)*. Oh, Daya! I've gone mad from the danger!

DAYA. No, you have not. He has many manly charms. He could love you.

RECHA. I don't know, Daya. I'm—reeling. I'm very concerned about all of this. There's a lot more involved in this sort of thing than one might think.

DAYA. Let nature take its course. And then you—and I— can go back to our own people.

RECHA. Is it right? For a Jew to love a Christian? You must think it's right, if you encourage me to love the Templar.

DAYA. Oh, merciful mother in heaven! If I could only talk. Hush. You sleep now.

*(DAYA leaves. RECHA sleeps. NATHAN comes up to DAYA.)*

NATHAN. How is my daughter?

DAYA. Your daughter?

NATHAN. May the day never come when I can't claim her as my daughter.

DAYA. At the price of my conscience.

NATHAN. Oh, is the price that high?

DAYA. You're a good man, Nathan, but—

NATHAN. A Jew nonetheless?

DAYA. You know what I mean.

NATHAN. I'm afraid I do. We need the young to dream the dreams we haven't dared. Recha is my daughter. I educated her in the classical trivium—

DAYA. Aha! The trivium! Very suspect, that!

NATHAN. —of logic, grammar, and rhetoric, in the service of piety. Don't you now fill her mind with your superstitious angels and your tin-pot guilty secrets. How is she?

DAYA (smiling). Oh. I would say…much better.


## SCENE 10

(The outskirts of Jerusalem. BONFILIO approaches CURD. BONFILIO continues to make his obsequious, hand-wringing gestures.)


CURD. If only I had something I could give you. I've got nothing—

BONFILIO. I was sent. By the Patriarch.

CURD. Why?

BONFILIO. To sound you out. You'll have to forgive me. I tend to grovel.

CURD. And for whom?

BONFILIO. Heraklios. That would be my guess. Because he's the one who sent me after you. He thinks God spared you so you might perform great deeds.

CURD. Such as?

BONFILIO. The Patriarch says that from time to time Saladin travels, practically alone. This is such an uncomfortable job.

CURD. I would hope so!

BONFILIO. What would be easier—the Patriarch says—than to grab him on his way? And cut him down? You tremble in disgust?

CURD. Do you know what I owe to Saladin?

BONFILIO. Well—the Patriarch, he's aware of it—and yet, God and the Order of Templars—

CURD. Neither calls for savagery!

BONFILIO. But the Patriarch thinks—what looks like savagery to you, and to me, may not look like that to God.

CURD. Enough. Does the Patriarch know why Saladin spared my life?

BONFILIO. You reminded Saladin of his long-dead brother Assad. So Saladin's pardon is nothing more than a whim. *(Wringing his hands.)* This is the Patriarch speaking.

CURD. I broke a truce. Took a chance. Lost the fight! By the rules of war I'm dead. I don't own my life anymore! *(Slamming the flat of his hand against his chest.)* Whose life is this? I don't know. And these arms have held a young woman in the middle of a furnace. And all this is happening in Jerusalem. Home of the Holy. But I don't see any holy. Where's the Holy? Spineless priest, I came here to find God! Off Cyprus, I lashed a burning ship to

an enemy vessel! I burned them hissing into the water!
My commander said I was brave! But I could see no de-
ity in the hissing water! I'd become a brute through my
search for God. But then He shows up as a maiden melt-
ing in the flames! The flash of Saladin's scimitar, in-
stead of killing, gives birth to me! Then Heraklios calls
this act of grace a whim so I can kill compliant with his
needs! By the Holy Sepulchre, my blood begins to boil
at this evil logic! So go, before I revert to type!

BONFILIO. Peace. I go. *(Aside.)*
      Than when I left more gay
      Do I return to hovel.
      My master's scheming plans
      Border close to lethal.
      We people of the cloth
      Are much too prone to grovel.


*(Exit BONFILIO. NATHAN appears. He approaches
CURD.)*


NATHAN. Excuse me!

CURD. What, Jew, what?

NATHAN. May I speak with you?

CURD *(starting to leave)*. Can I avoid it?

NATHAN. Stay. Don't brush me off with hauteur and inso-
      lence when you've bound me to you forever.

CURD. You owe me nothing. Did I know she was your
      daughter? It was my duty to help. Besides, my life was
      just a burden to me. I leapt at the chance to risk it, to
      lose it. Even if only for a Jewess.

NATHAN. Nobly detestable! You can't deceive me.
      You're modest—

CURD. I'm not modest. I'm a Christian who doesn't like Jews.

NATHAN. —and to escape my admiration you try to hide your goodness behind amateurish insults. You're a stranger and a prisoner, so let me be blunt. Tell me, command me. What can I do for you?

CURD. Nothing.

NATHAN. I am a rich man. Why refuse what I have to offer?

CURD. Very well. When my cape is worn out, I'll come to you and borrow fabric for a new one. Don't look so alarmed! It's still holding up. Though *(gesturing)* here, it's singed.

NATHAN *(reaching for that stained part of the cape, pondering it)*. Strange how a blemish tells more about the man than his own tongue. I will kiss—that spot! Oh, forgive me!—I didn't want to do that.

CURD. What?

NATHAN. I soiled it further with a tear.

CURD. Oh, that's nothing! It's been battered in trenches during ladder launch.

NATHAN. Send the cape to my daughter Recha.

CURD. Why?

NATHAN. So she can press her lips to this spot. *(CURD is silent in his frustration and embarrassment. NATHAN approaches him and puts his hand on his shoulder.)* It's hard work being churlish. I remember. I was churlish when I was young. I see right through you and down into the ground you're standing on. I know how decent people think. I find them in every country I visit.

CURD. But all these people are different?

NATHAN. Oh, in color and dress, yes. But such differences don't amount to much.

CURD. So you say, but who first came up with differences? Which people first called itself the chosen ones? I despise that arrogance! An arrogance that the Jews bequeathed to Christian and Muslim. So that now all three claim that their faith is the true faith. And they find ways to force that faith on the weeping Holy Land. And when did this raving madness—I have the best way to the best God—reveal itself more cruelly than in these religious wars, in the shocking here and now, in the Holy Land? Ah! If people want to be blind, what do I care! *(CURD starts to leave.)*

NATHAN. Don't go! Don't. The two of us must become friends! Yes, we're Christian, Jew and Muslim. And we're all God's creatures. All of us are human.

CURD. Human! What an idea to find in this disturbing holy land!

NATHAN. Well, you disturb me! My daughter owes you her life. And you make me feel that I've wasted mine!

CURD. You? Nathan the Wise? How?

NATHAN. I should have worked to stop these religious wars. Templar. I am a man. I judge nothing human alien to me. Do I detect in you a kindred spirit?

CURD. I've had too much of the human! I took the cross, vowed celibacy, to find God! But I've done nothing but kill. We've buried our dead with their living horses neighing in the graves!

NATHAN. The human is a dimension of divinity. You're young. You have the fire and imagination to find and touch the divine.

CURD. I did! In your burning home! In Recha! Nathan!—
Your hand!— I'm ashamed I misjudged you.

NATHAN. It's petty minds that rarely are misjudged.

CURD. But rare minds are never forgotten. *(CURD extends his hand. NATHAN takes it.)* Nathan, we have to become friends!

NATHAN. We are already. How delighted Recha will be! What happy prospects for the future! I want you to meet Recha!

CURD. I was terrified of her. *(NATHAN smiles. CURD smiles back.)* Now I want to meet her.

*(DAYA enters.)*

DAYA. Nathan! *(To CURD.)* Sir.

NATHAN. This is Daya.

DAYA. My honor, noble knight. *(To NATHAN.)* The sultan summons you. Go straightaway. What can he want?

NATHAN. Tell his messenger I shall attend the sultan immediately.

DAYA *(making the sign of the cross)*. God have mercy!

NATHAN. He will. Even in the sultan's palace. Go.

DAYA *(with a demure smile to CURD)*. *Et comment allez-vous, monsieur? (Exit DAYA.)*

CURD. My life's a gift from Saladin.

NATHAN. And so a gift to me. You will meet Recha in the hour after evensong. She awaits you.

CURD. Until that expectant hour.

NATHAN. And your name?

CURD. Curd von Stauffen.

NATHAN *(startled)*. Von Stauffen? That's one of the great houses of Germany.

CURD. Yes, it is. *(NATHAN stares at CURD.)* Nathan, are
   you well?

NATHAN. Yes, yes. I'm fine.

CURD. Thank you, Nathan. I wait impatient for evensong.
   *(Exit CURD.)*

NATHAN *(following him with his eyes. Amazed. To himself).* He has my friend von Filnek's stature. And he has
   von Stauffen's name. Strange. But, brains, awake. I must
   bring an alert soul to Saladin.


## SCENE 11

*(In the palace of SALADIN.)*

SITTAH. His pack animals trot on every route and cross
   every desert. In every port his ships ride at anchor. This
   one man, Nathan—

*(Enter HERAKLIOS.)*

HERAKLIOS. Is said to have found and explored the
   graves of David and Solomon. Is said to know secret
   codes to crack the seals of those graves and extract enor-
   mous treasures from those holy sites. Hence his great
   wealth. Wealth he gives to the poor, but refuses to
   church and mosque.

SALADIN. Welcome, Heraklios.

SITTAH. Patriarch, welcome.

HERAKLIOS. Princess Sittah, let old enmities fade.

SITTAH. I extend nothing but courtesy.

HERAKLIOS. I come in peace, to protect the peace.

SITTAH. You will find me reasonable, Patriarch.

SALADIN. To business.

HERAKLIOS. We begin with the area of agreement. There is one God.

SALADIN. Jew, Christian, and Muslim are People of the Book.

HERAKLIOS. All men must live secure in their own faiths—

SALADIN. —if God is to be served—

HERAKLIOS. —and if you, Saladin, are to govern.

SITTAH. All men and women. The Koran requires absolute spiritual and moral equality of the sexes.

HERAKLIOS. Agreed. All men and women. That is what I meant.

SITTAH. Of course it was.

SALADIN. The Koran states there is to be no compulsion in religion. Non-negotiable.

HERAKLIOS. Agreed. Each may assert his own. But, by the same token, no one may attack Christianity or Islam.

SALADIN. Or Judaism.

HERAKLIOS. Agreed. Anyone who asserts that either Islam or Christianity is not the true faith shall die.

SALADIN. Or Judaism.

HERAKLIOS. Why?

SALADIN. Because I am Saladin.

HERAKLIOS. Agreed.

SITTAH. There shall be no appeasement. No bootlicking. No apostasy. Anyone who denies his own faith shall die.

SALADIN. Agreed.

HERAKLIOS. Agreed. Then our business is finished. I bid you good day, and wish you the blessings of—peace.

SITTAH. As long as the truce holds.

HERAKLIOS. Those are matters military. I am a church-man. My thoughts are on higher things. *(HERAKLIOS is about to exit.)*

SITTAH. You were involved enough in my marriage, and my dowry, the military port of Akka.

HERAKLIOS. I ruled within my authority. Saladin, I have your oath?

SALADIN. You do.

HERAKLIOS. It is settled then. *(HERAKLIOS starts to leave.)* Oh, by the way, one addition. When there is a legal case that does not involve Muslims or the Shariah, the law of the Christian church shall be binding if the matter relates to the Christian faith.

SITTAH. It's a sound precept.

SALADIN. This troubles me.

SITTAH. It's a small matter.

SALADIN. The tiny gossamer of a midge's wing can be the mother of mischief.

SITTAH. The political powers are Muslim and Christian. Trust me.

SALADIN. Very well. Agreed.


*(Enter NATHAN.)*


NATHAN. I come at your summons, O Saladin.

SALADIN. Come closer! Don't be afraid!

NATHAN. May fear be what your enemies feel. My respects, Princess Sittah. Peace be with you, O Patriarch.

SALADIN. You are Nathan the Wise.

NATHAN. No.

SALADIN. The people call you Nathan the Wise.

NATHAN. True. But I'm rich. So I think they mean Nathan the Smart.

SALADIN. Can you teach me anything that would free me from these wars?

NATHAN. What laws have you made for the truce?

HERAKLIOS. He who denies his own religion shall die, as shall he who says that Christianity, Judaism or Islam is not the truc faith.

NATHAN. That will not make for spirited conversation in Jerusalem.

HERAKLIOS. You could, for example, right now give a defense of Judaism.

NATHAN. And what if my defense is too successful? Do I lose my head?

HERAKLIOS. Or you could discuss the attributes of God, such as existence and perfection.

NATHAN. But can we talk about Adonai as we talk about other matters?

SALADIN. So transcendent is God that we can talk about Him in parables only.

HERAKLIOS *(to NATHAN)*. What do you think?

NATHAN. I think that whereof we cannot speak, thereof we must sing.

HERAKLIOS. But tell me what you think the true God is. It comes to mind to ask, does God resemble any created being?

NATHAN *(smiles)*. As we are not in a court of law, you cannot compel me to reply. *(To SALADIN.)* Noble Saladin, I can teach you nothing. But, you can learn all things.

SITTAH. How?

NATHAN. Return to the spirit of the Prophet and the first four rightly guided caliphs. Listen to the Islamic hadith.

SALADIN. And what does the Islamic hadith say, O Jewish sage?

NATHAN. "Reflect upon God's creation but not upon his nature or you will perish."

SALADIN. I am more than content.

SITTAH *(circling to him)*. Nathan, you're a tradesman.

NATHAN. I'm a businessman.

SITTAH. What's the difference?

NATHAN. Initiative.

SITTAH. Let me show you something. *(From a jewel case SITTAH takes a gold ring with a braided tassel. The stone of the ring is an opal.)* This is the dynastic ring of our father, Ayyub. He gave it to our brother Assad, now dead. Every day since Assad rode away I have studied this ring under the Greek optic glass. I have made portraits of its every mood—every sunburst of its curious rainbow opal. Generations of our family, including Saladin and myself, have woven our history in code into this tassel to guarantee that this is the one, true Ayyubite ring. Nathan, what is the value of the ring?

*(NATHAN studies the ring carefully. He is shocked at what he sees.)*

NATHAN *(with great self-control)*. The ring is priceless.

SALADIN. What do you mean?

NATHAN. The concept of price has no meaning in relation to this ring.

SALADIN. Clarify.

NATHAN. Are your own ideas immediately perceived in your mind?

SITTAH. Yes.

NATHAN. The worth of this ring is likewise immediate. There is no medium of price.

SITTAH. Thank you. I begin to understand why they call you Nathan the Wise.

NATHAN *(to SALADIN)*. You are a great and chivalric Islamic ruler. To help you end the religious wars, I freely offer you ten millions of dinars for use at your discretion.

HERAKLIOS. There's not that much in Jerusalem!

NATHAN. With the arrival of my caravan, there is.

SALADIN. And what do you ask in return, to protect your loan?

NATHAN. It's not a loan. It's a gift outright. You have the power. Improve the world.

SALADIN. There are no terms?

NATHAN. Of course there are. Severe terms.

SALADIN. You say "severe" to me, to Saladin?

NATHAN. Yes.

SALADIN. What are these severe terms?

NATHAN. That you submit to the will of God.

HERAKLIOS. Whose God?

NATHAN. We agree there's only one. *(Beat.)*

SALADIN. Your offer is accepted.

NATHAN. Yesterday you spared the Templar. Last night he saved the life of my only living child, my daughter. Thank you. *(Beat.)* Our business is at an end?

SALADIN. There's just this. *(SALADIN extends his hand to NATHAN. The two men shake hands.)*

NATHAN. Honor to you, Patriarch of a holy faith. Princess Sittah, I go in the name of Allah, the merciful, the compassionate. Salaam alaykum.

SITTAH. Shalom. *(Exit NATHAN.)*

HERAKLIOS. All we agreed to will be bound by your oath?

SALADIN. It will. A charter will be drawn for our seals and sent to you.

HERAKLIOS. You know that your ring is the true one. I know that my faith is the true one.

SALADIN. Farewell.

HERAKLIOS. Farewell, Sultan, and Lady Sittah. *(Exit HERAKLIOS.)*

SITTAH. I want to know more of this Nathan, his daughter and her savior. Why did you spare that one Templar?

SALADIN. You'll see.

*(CURD strides in.)*

SALADIN *(cont'd)*. Here he comes unannounced.

SITTAH. Into the presence of the sultan! How dare he! *(CURD sees SITTAH and bows.)* So, this is the—

CURD. Lady Sittah, Curd von Stauffen, at your service.

*(SITTAH looks at CURD and stops speaking. Beat.)*

SALADIN. You were saying, Sittah?

SITTAH *(slowly)*. I was saying, so this is the daring revolutionary youth.

SALADIN. Oh. How foolish of me. I thought you were going to say let's cut off his head at the earliest possible convenience.

CURD. I am your prisoner, Sultan.

SALADIN. I don't think so. What do you think, Lady Sittah, woman of steel? Lover of Akka?

SITTAH *(to CURD)*. I want to hear you talk.

CURD. Talk?

SITTAH. Yes. *(She makes a little talking gesture.)* Talk.

CURD. I am here to offer you my service.

*(SALADIN and SITTAH exchange looks.)*

SALADIN. Go on. Offer service.

CURD *(a little flustered, suspecting he is being mocked)*. Only, Sultan, do not expect excessive thanks from me for having spared my life. My character and my position won't allow it. Having said that, my life is at your service.

SALADIN. Do you see?

SITTAH. His voice! His face! And his impetuous manner!

SALADIN. You are my Assad, heart and soul. Where have you been during all these years?

SITTAH *(circling CURD)*. What cave have you slept in? What genie has kept you fresh and fragrant? *(To SALADIN.)* This could be our brother Assad, had he escaped from age!

CURD. I know no Assad.

SITTAH. This hurts while it pleases!

SALADIN *(to CURD)*. You are much like our brother Assad.

CURD. I don't know why this is, but—it's strange—my soul has dreamt of this.

SITTAH. You make my soul dream as well. And I thought it had died. I feel like singing! From the flat roofs of Jerusalem!

SALADIN *(to CURD)*. Let's put what your soul has dreamt of to the test. Will you stay with us? As Christian or as Muslim! In white cape or in caftan. I've never asked that every tree grow the same bark.

CURD. That's what makes you the Improver of the World.

SALADIN. Oh, I'm a great failure at that. But, as a start, let me improve us. What do you say, oh mirror of Assad! We're halfway there.

CURD *(impetuously)*. All the way!

SALADIN *(looks at SITTAH; offering him his hand)*. Two hands, one man?

CURD *(accepting it)*. One man! I'm yours. And of my free will I'll give you back more than you could ever have taken with your scimitar.

SITTAH. You rescued the daughter of Nathan.

CURD. I did.

SITTAH. I'm looking at a troubled young man.

CURD. No.

SITTAH. Am I not?

CURD. No.

SITTAH. Give me of your own free will what I could not take with a scimitar.

CURD. Oh, Lady! I am troubled. I am torn. I have taken vows.

SITTAH. Tell me. The young woman. What is her name?

SALADIN. Answer Lady Sittah. She means you no harm.

CURD. Oh, don't give me a new life and then make me miserable in it!

*(SALADIN and SITTAH cannot help looking at each other upon each of CURD's outbursts.)*

SITTAH. I won't make you miserable. Tell me.

CURD. Recha.

SITTAH *(gently)*. Recha.

CURD. Recha! What I did for her, I did—because I did it. *(A glance between SITTAH and SALADIN confirms that this is a familiar logic. They also know that CURD is suffering.)* I'm a celibate, Lady Sittah!

SITTAH *(gently)*. So am I.

CURD. I don't know what to do. Oh, I am ashamed, Sultan!

SALADIN. Ashamed? That a Jewish girl impressed you so? Muhammad—peace be upon him—married a Jewish wife. Are you greater than Muhammad?

SITTAH. Go to her.

CURD. Could I? Go to her?

SITTAH. This is Jerusalem. It is a holy land. The human soul is alive in Jerusalem.

SALADIN. Listen to this gentle lady. *(CURD kneels before SALADIN.)* Oh, no, Templar. There will be no European hand-kissing here. Surrender your whole being not to the sultan but to the Creator.

*(CURD rises, looks steadily at SALADIN and SITTAH, and strides out. SALADIN looks at his sister, sits, and tents his hands. SITTAH is gazing after CURD.)*

SALADIN *(cont'd)*. Akka is such a lovely town. Known for its healthy and diverting locales: Bloodgate, Accursed Tower, Portal of the Evil Step. You really must visit it sometime, Sittah.

SITTAH. I have to see this young woman, Recha.

SALADIN. Why, sister?

SITTAH. Because she is loved.

*(LIGHTS OFF SALADIN and SITTAH.)*

## SCENE 12

*(Enter RECHA from one side. CURD from the other.)*

CURD. Hello.
RECHA. Hello. *(Pause.)*
CURD. My name is Curd.
RECHA. I am Recha. *(Pause.)*
CURD. Von Stauffen.
RECHA. Von Nathan.
CURD. A Templar.
RECHA. A virgin.
CURD. A Christian.
RECHA. A Jew. *(Pause.)*
CURD. A man.
RECHA. A virgin.
CURD. We did that.
RECHA. No, we didn't.
CURD. Thought we did.
RECHA. No, we didn't. *(Pause.)*
CURD. Curd.
RECHA. Recha.
CURD. Good.
RECHA. Better.
CURD. Hello.
RECHA. Hello. *(Pause.)*
CURD. I don't care about your beauty.
RECHA. Could we go back?
CURD. No. I don't care about your beauty.

RECHA. Well, we're pretty much even there. I don't think about it much. In fact I didn't know I had it. Until just now. When you mentioned it. I'm glad to know I have it. What you have said is—somewhat flattering. But, Curd, I must say, it is not overwhelmingly flattering. Curd, if you don't care about it, why bring it up at all? Curd, did you, by any chance, think about what you were going to say to me when we met?

CURD. Yes.

RECHA. And what was your plan?

CURD. I planned to say I couldn't think of anything to say. Not much there, I admit. But it was better than casting my eyes down and spitting. But when I saw you, your loveliness caused changes in me. Made my throat dry. So I decided to tell the truth.

RECHA. This being—?

CURD & RECHA. I don't care about your beauty.

RECHA. So. I suppose I'm in fairly good shape. It turns out I'm beautiful but I don't have a suitor.

CURD. Oh, yes you do. Me. You glow from inside. You glowed brighter than the ebbed bottom coals in the fire I pulled you from. You lit up my cape like a white jewel. I laughed at the fire when I saw you. When I saw you I said, "This woman will not burn. I'll rip this place down with my bare hands before I'll let this incandescent one, this gentle beauty burn. She has light enough of her own. I'll smash this place." I said. And I gathered you up.

RECHA. Oh, yes you did, Curd. You did. Gather me up. All of me.

CURD. But. You make me want. But. Not— Not what a fighting man lusts after when he's mad with time and wounds and sees a woman. You make me want—

RECHA. What?

CURD. Help me. Help me understand what I want.

RECHA. I want to help you. Why did you come to the Holy Land?

CURD. I don't know. I don't have a brain to beat on or a word to throw at a dog.

RECHA. You have a fine brain. Why did you come?

CURD. I didn't come to speak the words—

*(DAYA enters, unseen. When she sees the two together, she listens quietly.)*

CURD *(cont'd)*. "I love you." *(DAYA exits, smiling.)*

RECHA. Then why?

CURD. I came to fight for God. We strap raw meat under our saddles, Recha, and ride for days. When we arrive it's cooked. In sweat. We camp. We lay siege. We go up walls. At the top I meet swords and scimitars. They meet the strength of my right arm. I do it. It's my duty. But does God need me to fight for Him? So my hunger changed. I no longer want to fight for God. I want to find God. I wept when I realized that is why I came to this land.

RECHA. To the Holy Land.

CURD. The arid land became the Holy Land when I went into that fire, Recha. And found you. And so I say it's not your beauty but it's you—that—I—love. *(Pause. In what follows the two young people come closer and closer to each other.)*

RECHA. I am not prepared for this.

CURD. Nor am I.

RECHA. This is hard.

CURD. Yes.

RECHA. This is too big. Too fast. Not right. *(Beat.)*

CURD. Just right.

RECHA. Just right.

CURD. I want to talk to you. Time without end.

RECHA. About?

CURD. Not love. Gold light on turrets. White light on the water. The milkweed sail. The fishes of the air.

RECHA. The birds of the deep. I see. About everything.

CURD. Yes, Recha.

RECHA. Curd? Maybe sometimes God is a spark in a dark place.

CURD. Maybe that's a part of it. I think so.

RECHA. I do care about your beauty.

CURD. That will pass.

RECHA. I probably shouldn't.

CURD. Who cares?

RECHA. You're nobler than I am.

CURD. Who cares?

RECHA. Because you don't care about my beauty and I do care about yours.

CURD. But? *(Beat.)*

RECHA. But it's you—that—I—love.

*(LIGHTS down.)*

## SCENE 13

*(AL-HAFI encounters DAYA, who is sweeping up debris from the steps of Nathan's house.)*

AL-HAFI. Run off with me to the Ganges.

DAYA. Go along, I have no time for your twirling and your schematisms.

AL-HAFI. Jerusalem is a wasteland of barren minds plotting empty revenges on the surface of a thistle. Come with me to India, by the river Ganges. Trade the dust of your dress for the perfume of a sari. Come away with me, beauteous Daya, to a life of indolence, heavy fragrant air, mystery, magic, and chess.

DAYA. I've told you over and over again, Al-Hafi. A Mussulman beggar is no match for a good Christian woman.

AL-HAFI. Answer love with love. Doesn't my passion make your heart gentle?

DAYA. It makes my fingers itch to give you a good rap with my broom.

AL-HAFI. Daya, oh beautiful Daya, holding and withholding yourself from my amorous embraces year after year—child, maid, and matron. When you were a green grape, you refused me. When you were a ripe grape, you said me nay. Now, oh Daya, in our old age, don't deny me a bite of your raisin. *(DAYA responds with blows of her broom, chasing AL-HAFI off.)*

DAYA. Oh! I'll teach you, you won-ton, lusty *laissez-faire* foreign rascal! Love is not found in markets or in hallways! Love has always loved to live in Anjou! *(DAYA makes a punctuating sweep of her broom. Her legs give way and she collapses on the floor.)* My knees! *(She looks where AL-HAFI has disappeared. She is utterly dismayed to realize—)* My knees went weak!

*(LIGHTS DOWN.)*

**INTERMISSION**

# ACT II

## SCENE 1

*(SITTAH and RECHA enter at opposite sides of a palace garden.)*

RECHA. Lady Sittah!

SITTAH. Recha, walk with me in the garden. *(They walk.)* In these cool shades the flower-killing simoom wind can never reach.

RECHA. This is an honor.

SITTAH. For me.

RECHA. Call me your child.

SITTAH. Hardly. *(Beat.)* That's why I've asked you to walk with me. Because you're a woman. Because I want to know what kind of woman is loved. You think I am a great lady. But I'm not. I am a mule. *(Pulls at her hair.)* See? Short mane. Stubborn. Barren. Recha, there are things that must be done while you are young. The years slide away, olive-oiled with pleasant resentment and suddenly you're old. Recha, you are loved. What is it like?

RECHA. I haven't got the slightest idea. But my heart's full.

SITTAH *(caressing RECHA's hair)*. Being near you is like tasting the wine made before Adam. Speak to me. *(A confidence.)* Recha. I once loved a prince.

*(LIGHTS CROSS-FADE to:)*

## SCENE 2

*(A plaza in Jerusalem. CURD waits for NATHAN.)*

CURD *(restlessly pacing back and forth)*. I am a Templar—bound to chastity—and in love. A Christian loves a Jew.

*(NATHAN enters.)*

CURD *(cont'd)*. Promise me—that I shall see her always.
NATHAN. What am I to make of this?
CURD *(embracing him fervently)*. Father!
NATHAN. Young man!
CURD. I love Recha. Let me be your son!
NATHAN. Dear young man!
CURD *(stepping back, stung to the quick)*. You refuse to call me son? I love her.
NATHAN. Dear, dear friend!
CURD. It's because I'm Christian, isn't it!
NATHAN. I've got to know more about you.
CURD. Know more! Is curiosity all you can feel?
NATHAN. I knew a von Stauffen once. His name was Conrad.
CURD. That was my father's name. I'm named after him. Curd is short for Conrad.
NATHAN. But the Conrad I knew was a Templar. A—

CURD. Celibate? He could still have been my father. He lived in times of war. Nathan! This is so unlike you. What happened to "There are no differences"?

NATHAN. I have my reasons for delay. It hurts me but—I can't speak the word "son" to you. Not yet.

*(NATHAN exits. DAYA enters.)*

CURD. Daya! I love Recha!

DAYA. I know.

CURD. I want to marry her. But Nathan rejects me. *(Bitter.)* A mere Christian isn't good enough for his Jewish daughter.

DAYA. That's not it.

CURD. Of course it is! And he has the power of a father.

DAYA. No, he doesn't.

CURD. Of course he does!

DAYA. If I could only talk. If I could only talk. *(She makes up her mind.)* I *will* talk. *(Beat.)* Recha is not Jewish. She's a Christian.

CURD. You're inventing this!

DAYA. She is a Christian child. Born of Christian parents. Baptized.

CURD. And Nathan?

DAYA. Not her father! To hide this truth cost me many bloody tears over the years.

CURD. Just brought her up as his daughter? Brought her up Jewish, though she is a Christian?

DAYA. Yes, yes! That's it!

CURD. And never told her that she was born a Christian, not a Jew?

DAYA. Never!

CURD. And why do you reveal this now?

DAYA. I've got to get home! When you take Recha off to Europe, take me, too! *(Urgently.)* Because if I stay here— *(Tapping her knees.)* My soul is in danger!

*(Exit DAYA. Enter HERAKLIOS and BONFILIO.)*

HERAKLIOS. What a delight. To meet the Templar. Such a brave young man. And still so young. With God's help, he can still develop.

CURD. I am troubled, O Patriarch, and seek your counsel.

HERAKLIOS. I'll give it gladly. But, it should be followed.

CURD. But not blindly?

HERAKLIOS. It is quite right to make use of one's God-given reason. But not in every case. Oh, no! For instance: should God so honor us as to reveal through one of his angels—perhaps, a servant of His word—a way to fortify the strength of Christianity and the glory of the Church, who are we to look for reason in a command by Him, who gifted us with reason? And who are we to measure the eternal laws of glorious heaven by our small rules of arrogant honor? *(Beat.)* Your question?

CURD. Let's assume, Reverend Father, a Jew had a child, an only child—a girl, whom he brought up in virtue, a girl he loved more than his own soul. And she, in turn, was devoted to him as her father. And now let's say it comes out that she's not the daughter of the Jew. And let's assume the girl's a Christian!

HERAKLIOS. Baptized?

CURD. Yes, but brought up Jewish by this Jew who claims her as his daughter. Tell me, Reverend Father, what would the proper course of action be?

HERAKLIOS. I shudder at the thought! But, let me ask you this. Did you imagine this or did it really happen? And is it in fact happening at this very moment?

CURD. What does it matter?

HERAKLIOS. Now, there you are! So very much mistaken about the role of reason in matters of spirituality. Indeed, it matters greatly! For, if we're dealing with mere conjecture, there's no need to spend more time on it. But. Should there be more to it. Should this be fact, happening right here in our diocese— Well, then—

CURD. What then?

HERAKLIOS. The Jew would be subject to the full extent of papal law reserved for such a crime.

CURD. Which is?

HERAKLIOS. The law will on the instant condemn a Jew who induced a Christian to leave her faith to be burnt at the stake.

CURD. Burnt! But what if the child would have perished, if the Jew had not taken pity on it?

HERAKLIOS. No matter. Why, pray, does this Jew presume to do the work of God? Could God Himself not have saved the child, if He so chose?

BONFILIO. But maybe God saved the child, through the Jew.

HERAKLIOS. It doesn't matter. The Jew must burn.

CURD. It was just a hypothesis.

HERAKLIOS. Every hypothesis hungers to be a thesis.

CURD. None of this took place.

HERAKLIOS. You forget, I've heard many a confession. I know what is frightened evasion and what is painful and even dangerous truth. *(Exit HERAKLIOS.)*

CURD. What have I done? I've got to get to Saladin.

BONFILIO. Templar, you're quite a young fool. I hope you're not like the reckless mountaineer. Whose shout brings down the avalanche.

*(Exit BONFILIO and CURD. CROSS-FADE to RECHA and SITTAH.)*

### SCENE 3

RECHA. I am myself amazed how such a tempest in my heart can so suddenly be still. I've been with him, Lady Sittah. Seen his green and glinting eye, his firm jaw, up close, just as once I felt his power sweep me up and protect me from the flames. Oh, he's steel to the back! The Templar is a handsome fellow, I'll say it right out to anyone, and as good a man as bears a hide. But. Oh, I love him. Yes, I do. And yet. Oh, he is a man, all right, so much as to make me tremble. Such male authority in his voice. A youthful gravel. Strong. But. Oh, I want to be with him, share the sweet air of youth with him. Find out adventures!

SITTAH. And yet—

RECHA. My knees. It's my knees, don't you see? I'm foolish. I'm confused. But my knees, my knees, my dearest lady, are perfectly firm.

## SCENE 4

*(The palace of SALADIN. CURD rushes into the presence of SALADIN.)*

CURD. Oh Sultan! Help Nathan.

SALADIN. What's happened to him?

CURD. I've endangered him! I've brought upon him the wrath of—

*(SITTAH enters with HERAKLIOS.)*

SITTAH. Heraklios has urgent business, O Sultan.

HERAKLIOS. Saladin.

CURD. Don't listen to him! It's a fiction!

HERAKLIOS *(icy look at CURD)*. The girl Recha, whom Nathan calls his daughter, is a baptized Christian child and not his own. Nathan has reared her as a Jew. By the laws, by you newly proclaimed, this case is subject to my authority.

SALADIN. How so?

HERAKLIOS. Wherever the law of the Christian church does not conflict with Islamic laws, it shall be binding in all matters relating to the Christian faith. This is a matter of Christian and Jew.

SALADIN. There must be a trial.

HERAKLIOS. Its result is a foregone conclusion.

SITTAH. Why?

HERAKLIOS. Because it is well known that Nathan does not lie.

SALADIN. What is the penalty for Nathan's act, under papal and imperial law?

HERAKLIOS. It is a simple penalty, for a major crime. His wealth is forfeit to the Church. The Jew must burn. *(Exit HERAKLIOS.)*

CURD. What have I done?

SALADIN. Calm down, Christian! You've surrendered Nathan to a religious fanatic! Who will now use me to take his revenge. You've put my power into the hands of Heraklios. *(SALADIN calls out.)* Guards! Seize and imprison Nathan!

*(Tableau of NATHAN being led into prison. As he walks, he sings wailing, cantorial MUSIC. SOUND of prison doors closing.)*

## SCENE 5

*(RECHA and CURD.)*

CURD. I'm such a fool. I caused this.

RECHA. Oh, Curd! Daya tells me he's not my father. That's like saying these hands aren't my hands. She tells me Judaism is not my tradition. Oh, Curd! Heraklios has trapped Nathan!

CURD. We've got to help him. Together. And we will.

RECHA. How, Curd?

CURD. We'll break him out of prison.

RECHA. Very well. We will. Nathan is my tradition.

## SCENE 6

*(NATHAN in prison. He is puttering about with a small pot and a fire, preparing a meal. CURD appears at the cell window, pulls the bars apart and leaps into NATHAN's cell.)*

CURD. Come! I have two horses. We'll fight our way out!

NATHAN. How many horses?

CURD. Two!

NATHAN. And once more the method of escaping?

CURD. Combat!

NATHAN. Ah! Combat. Escape without me. *(Beat.)* I'm baking some bread. Would you like some?

CURD. Baking bread? How can you do that?

NATHAN. Well, you get yourself a capped ceramic pot, a foot and a half high. You put strips of dough along the edges of the pot, and stick the whole thing in the fire.

CURD. I mean, at a time like this?

NATHAN. A time like this? This is suppertime. A very good time to make bread.

CURD. I betrayed you.

NATHAN *(calmly)*. Well, there was a lull in the fighting. What else was there to do?

CURD. Whoever gave Recha her life, you will remain her true father into all eternity.

NATHAN. I have nothing against eternity. I just want to see if I can think of a way to enjoy a little more of the good old here and now.

CURD. If I imagine a mere Christian girl, stripped of everything you have given her, what would I see? Nothing! There wouldn't be that strange charm that she now emanates.

NATHAN. Merciful heaven! Curd, you are a handful. From combat to emanations!

CURD. Let me rescue you!

NATHAN. No! But thank you, Curd.

*(Enter RECHA.)*

RECHA. Father! Are you all right?

NATHAN. Recha. Do you also have a rescue plan?

RECHA. Curd and I have planned your escape.

CURD. There's a tunnel!

NATHAN. There will be no escape.

RECHA. Father! I've heard a whirlwind of accusations! What's true and what's false?

NATHAN. What's true is that I love you. What's false I leave to my accusers.

RECHA. Am I your daughter?

NATHAN. I don't know. Are you? I did not beget you.

RECHA. Am I Christian?

NATHAN *(smiling)*. I don't know. Are you? You were baptized Christian.

RECHA. Why didn't you tell me? *(Pause.)*

NATHAN. Recha, there are some things that hurt so much don't ask me.

RECHA. So I'm not your daughter.

NATHAN. We'll find out tomorrow.

RECHA. What do you mean?

NATHAN. I mean it's good I'm here. In prison. That's why we're not going to escape. No fighting, no swords, no horses. It's good there will be a trial, for the crime of loving you so much it makes my heart break.

CURD. What will they charge against you?

NATHAN. Heraklios hungers to pose the unanswerable question. "What is the true faith?" Given the new laws, it's the same as murder to ask that question. If I say Judaism is the true faith—

RECHA. You die.

CURD. Attack on Islam.

RECHA. Attack on Christianity.

NATHAN. If I say Islam or Christianity—

CURD. You die.

RECHA. Denial of your faith.

NATHAN. If you love me, bring your imagination to this trial. Your daring. Your youth, in its generosity. I am only a man. I will come to my wits' end. When I do, I want to hear from you both. *(Looking inside the pot.)* Bread's done. So. Time to get to work. Templar, go out the way you came. Find the friar and tell him I need to see him now. Recha. Get word to Al-Hafi that he must go to the jewel casket of Saladin and "do what comes naturally."

RECHA. What does that mean?

NATHAN. He'll know. Tell him to bring "the result" to me. Along with the gold purse from my caravan. Recha, do you have that?

RECHA. Yes.

CURD. Maybe we should fight.

RECHA. No, we'll listen to Nathan.

NATHAN. Go. You that way, *(gesturing toward the window)* so they won't know you've been here, *(to RECHA)* and you by the door! Go!

*(RECHA and CURD exit. DAYA enters. She is carrying a long cloth.)*

DAYA *(solemnly)*. Nathan.

NATHAN. Daya! Just the person I wanted to see. And how is everything at home?

DAYA. Nathan. Time is short. Your trial is tomorrow. The Templar loves your Recha. Give her to him. That way, your sin, that I can hide no longer—

NATHAN. Hide? My dear Daya. It's right out there in the open. That's why I'm in here. It seems someone popped that little old secret.

DAYA. I beg you, give Recha to the Templar. That way, your sin, that is hidden no longer, will have an end.

NATHAN. And that's not the only thing.

DAYA. No Patriarch will dare threaten the bride of a Templar befriended by Saladin. The girl will be with Christians. And I'll be with her.

NATHAN. Yes, I know, and you'll all go to Europe. And I'll go from sinner to cinder.

DAYA. Nathan. I'm sorry I endangered you. So I made you a gift.

NATHAN. What is it?

DAYA *(sepulchrally)*. A shroud.

NATHAN. Daya. You are a little bundle of sunshine. Go. And take that mournful rag with you! *(Exit DAYA.)* The truth is, I don't feel in a light mood at all.

## SCENE 7

*(The palace of SALADIN. SITTAH is sitting at the chess-board. AL-HAFI enters and at first does not see her. He approaches the jewel casket. But then he sees SITTAH.)*

AL-HAFI. Most noble Princess. Please tell my master Saladin I have almost completed the transfer of Nathan's money to the vaults.

SITTAH. Very good, Al-Hafi.

AL-HAFI. May I? *(AL-HAFI moves a chess piece.)*

SITTAH. Al-Hafi. *(SITTAH makes a move.)* Have you ever loved? *(This stops AL-HAFI cold.)*

AL-HAFI. Yes. *(He makes a move.)*

SITTAH. And?

AL-HAFI. I don't know what to say.

SITTAH *(makes a move)*. Say the truth.

AL-HAFI. She rejects me. *(Makes a move.)* Check.

SITTAH *(makes a move)*. Why?

AL-HAFI. Because I am— *(Makes a move.)* Muslim. Mate. *(AL-HAFI hastens, but trips himself up and stumbles against the table on which the casket is placed.)* I am a clumsy wretch! My mind was on the game. And now like an arrow I go to serve Saladin.

*(Exit AL-HAFI. SITTAH stares at the chessboard.)*

## SCENE 8

*(NATHAN is in his cell, baking bread. We can't see any-
one else.)*

NATHAN. I couldn't bear it. Not to be her father any
more. *(Beat.)* Thank you for coming.
BONFILIO *(off)*. You've given me many gifts over the
years.
NATHAN. May I confess something to you?

*(BONFILIO comes out of the shadows.)*

BONFILIO. Not officially.
NATHAN. Not officially, of course. I'm concerned.
BONFILIO. You should be. Nature has fashioned us so
that we become wise at our own expense. Heraklios is a
formidable opponent. He has arranged the laws for this
very opportunity. But I can help.
NATHAN. I felt you might be able to, although I couldn't
tell you why.
BONFILIO. You've often slipped something into my
hands. A little money. A honey cake. I once slipped
something into your hands. Heraklios asked me to trace
you. Get something on you. And as I did, I realized that
I have played my part in your so-called unpardonable
sin. Do you recall, sixteen years ago, a horseman who
handed you a little girl only a few weeks old?
NATHAN. Yes.
BONFILIO. I am that horseman.
NATHAN. You?

BONFILIO. The gentleman who'd asked me to entrust the little girl to you was Wolf von Filnek.

NATHAN. He was my friend.

BONFILIO. Her mother had just died and von Filnek was called to Gaza. He couldn't take this little girl to war, and sent her to you.

NATHAN. That's right!

BONFILIO. Von Filnek fell in Askalon. He was an honorable man.

NATHAN. I owe him much! He saved me from being murdered for my views!

BONFILIO. Perhaps it would have been better, if Recha had been brought up Christian, by a Christian. But God is love. You gave the child love. She grew up healthy in your care. God would, I think, approve.

NATHAN. Can you tell me anything more about von Filnek or Recha's mother?

BONFILIO (maddeningly deliberate). Jew, Christian, and Muslim are People of the Book.

NATHAN (finding it harder to keep control). I know that. But tomorrow two of my fellow Booklovers are going to burn me to a decidedly single death!

BONFILIO (calmly). I myself cannot read. I hear it's harmful. (He draws a small prayer book from the folds of his robe.) Is the bread done?

NATHAN. What?

BONFILIO. The bread. Is it baked?

NATHAN. Yes, yes.

BONFILIO. May I have some?

NATHAN. Yes, of course. (NATHAN gives BONFILIO some bread. BONFILIO munches it contentedly.)

BONFILIO. A little low in leaven. This prayer book be-
longed to Wolf von Filnek. I took it from his body when
I buried him at Askalon. *(Rubbing his hands together.)* I
still have an arrow-tip, in the bone of my hand, from
Askalon. It's strange, Nathan, I can't remember which
side I fought on! This little book— *(BONFILIO hands
the prayer book to NATHAN.)* It's filled with his writing.
In Arabic. Good luck, Nathan. Winter's thunder is sum-
mer's wonder.

*(Exit BONFILIO. We hear the SLAMMING OF THE
JAIL DOOR.)*


## SCENE 9

*(The palace of SALADIN. RECHA is on her knees,
weeping.)*

SALADIN. What is the meaning of this, Sittah?
SITTAH. She's beside herself!
SALADIN. This is Recha? Our Nathan's daughter?
SITTAH. Yes. *(To RECHA.)* Pull yourself together, child!
The sultan stands before you.
RECHA *(on her knees to SALADIN)*. I won't get up! I
won't look upon the sultan's face! I won't gaze in won-
der at the reflection of eternal justice and kindness in his
eyes. I won't, unless—
SALADIN. Tell me, child.
RECHA. Unless you promise to leave me my father! It is-
n't blood that makes a father! O Saladin, Improver of
the World! Don't let them take Nathan from me!

SALADIN *(helping her get up)*. The real world is a stern world. My power is above my personal will. It's in the service of the law.

RECHA. How cruel!

SALADIN. If the worst happens, I will be your father.

RECHA. He is the best man among you!

SITTAH. Recha! Nathan is not your real father. All that counts is kith and kin, and the True Faith. You've already lost your true kin.

SALADIN. Child. I, too, have lost someone I dearly loved. Dear Recha, the sultan is bound by the law or there is no law. *(Calling.)* Let the trial of Nathan the Wise begin.

*(HERAKLIOS enters, attended by BONFILIO. DAYA enters. NATHAN enters, in chains. He looks weak and dejected. CURD runs in.)*

CURD. Unfair! Unfair, I say!

SALADIN. Silence, Templar! This is a trial at law. He who would weigh the wind must have a steady hand.

CURD. The laws condemn an innocent man!

NATHAN. I want you to use your mind. Not those strong arms.

SALADIN. Patriarch, what is your charge?

HERAKLIOS. That Nathan did raise the Christian child Recha as a Jew.

SALADIN. What proof have you?

HERAKLIOS. Mistress, step forward. *(DAYA comes forward.)* Your name and work?

DAYA. My name is Daya, and I have been Recha's nurse since her babyhood.

HERAKLIOS. Is Recha Christian?

DAYA. She is.

HERAKLIOS. How do you know this?

DAYA *(looking guiltily at NATHAN)*. Nathan told me. She was born of a German couple, the von Filneks. Christians.

HERAKLIOS. Return to your place.

DAYA. Forgive me, Nathan. I didn't know what I was doing.

HERAKLIOS. Return to your place. *(DAYA does so.)* You've done very well. By Saladin's proclamation, if there is no conflict with Islamic law, the law of the Church is binding.

SALADIN. This seems to be a matter between Jew and Christian, with no involvement of Muslims or Islam. What is the law of the Church?

HERAKLIOS. Burn the Jew.

SALADIN. Was that said by Jesus, may peace be upon Him?

HERAKLIOS. I know the law. And your inquiries, O Saladin, are irrelevant, as there is nothing of Islam in this case.

SALADIN. Nathan, what is your reply?

NATHAN. Sixteen years ago, a man gave me a baby girl. That girl was Recha. The man stands here.

SALADIN. Which is he?

NATHAN. This friar. *(A general sense of surprise among the onlookers, especially HERAKLIOS.)*

SALADIN. Friar Bonfilio, is this true?

BONFILIO. Yes, it is the truth, so help me God. I gave the child Recha to Nathan.

NATHAN. You gave her to me. I did not think to lose her after all these years of loving her.

HERAKLIOS. Whether you lose her or not is irrelevant. You admit she's Christian.

NATHAN. I admit her mother was Christian. *(To BON-FILIO.)* Who was her father?

BONFILIO. A soldier.

NATHAN. He was my friend. And what was his name?

BONFILIO. Wolf von Filnek.

HERAKLIOS. That's a German name. The father is Christian.

BONFILIO. No. The father wrote and spoke Arabic.

SALADIN. How do you know this?

BONFILIO. Before I became a man of the cloth, I was his servant.

NATHAN. What was his race, his religion?

BONFILIO. Wolf von Filnek was a Kurd from Kurdistan. He faithfully upheld the Five Pillars of Islam.

SALADIN. What are those, Bonfilio?

BONFILIO. Shahadah, prayer, zakat, fasting, and the hajj. Unswervingly observed. He was Muslim.

SALADIN. I am myself a Kurd. My father Ayyub was from Kurdistan. This case involves a Muslim who adopted a German name, Wolf von Filnek. Recha is a Muslim baptized Christian. The matter therefore comes under Muslim law. It comes, O Patriarch, under my jurisdiction. Heraklios' claim to judgment is denied.

HERAKLIOS. Nathan has raised a Muslim as a Jew.

NATHAN. It seems I've raised everyone as a Jew. Saladin, is that a crime in Muslim law? In either Koran, sunnah, or ijtihad?

SALADIN. It is not. The Shariah is tolerant.

NATHAN. And in the hadith, we learn that Muhammad, peace be upon him, said: "Seek knowledge, though it be in China." What if it be in Jerusalem? Among the Jews?

SALADIN. If knowledge is in Jerusalem, among the Jews, seek it there, with my blessing. Our proceedings are at an end.

*(Rejoicing begins but is cut short.)*

HERAKLIOS. No, they are not. During litigation I have the right to ask any question I wish.

CURD. I'll cut his head off!

SALADIN. A legal subtlety which I must overrule. You have that right. Heraklios, what further question could there be?

HERAKLIOS. Tell me, Nathan, since you are so wise, tell me, what faith, what law has made most sense to you?

NATHAN. Heraklios, I am a Jew.

HERAKLIOS. And I a Christian. Saladin is Muslim. But a man like you does not remain where the accident of birth has pinned him. If you are a Jew, it's because of insight, reasons, preference. You have chosen, and you have chosen for a reason. I want your reason. And my question to you is: which is the true faith? *(Pause.)*

SALADIN. Nathan. Be advised. The new laws state: Anyone who denies his own faith shall die. Anyone who says that Christianity, Judaism or Islam is not the true religion shall likewise die.

DAYA. Unfair! That question will kill him! That is unfair! Intolerable! It is spigoted!

SALADIN. Silence.

DAYA. Oh, that we were in Europe, where the winds are cool and all trials are fair!

NATHAN. In distant times, in the Orient, there lived a man who had inherited a ring of immeasurable worth. This ring had the power to make the one who wore it with conviction loved by God and humankind. Small wonder, then, that this man from the Orient never took off his ring and stipulated that this ring was to stay forever within his dynasty. He bequeathed the ring to his favorite son, who, in turn, was to bequeath the ring to his favorite son. And so on, down through time. The possessor of the ring was always to be the head of the dynasty, regardless of his rank in birth.

HERAKLIOS. I don't want to hear about a ring! Answer the question.

SALADIN. He's on trial. By Muslim law he has the right to frame his reply by any sound endeavor of the mind. This interests me. I have such a ring. You have seen it, Nathan. It is an opal.

NATHAN. Yes, I have seen it. And the ring in my story is an opal as well, reflecting myriad colors.

SITTAH. An opal!

NATHAN. This ring was handed down to a father of three sons. All three showed him respect and he loved all of them alike. But, when he met with any of his sons alone and that son poured out his heart to him, he wavered. At times he would consider this son or that worthiest of the ring. And at one time or another he managed to promise it to each of the three sons! Now—it comes time for this man to die. He is at a loss. It pains him to have to hurt two of his sons. What is he to do?

DAYA. Alas, poor man, he's lost. What a plight! What a fix. What a pickle.

NATHAN. In secret he arranges for an artist to fashion two more rings just like the original—

SITTAH. Impossible.

NATHAN. —and not to spare cost and effort to make them look in all aspects alike. The artist succeeds. When he brings him the rings, the father himself cannot distinguish between the original and its imitations. Relieved and glad at heart he calls for his sons, one by one alone. He gives each his blessing—and his ring—and dies.

DAYA. Oh, no!

NATHAN. The father dead, each son produced his ring, and clamored to be head of the dynasty. They quarreled, sued, fought. In vain. No son could prove that his was the true ring. Just as today no one can prove which is the true religion.

HERAKLIOS. But the religions are quite distinguishable. Down to the last detail. Like clothing, food and drink! Wine! Pork! Meat on Fridays!

NATHAN. These are all things indifferent. Each religion claims to be at its core the word of God made manifest to men and women.

SALADIN. Continue. Muhammad, may peace be upon him, said: "Difference of opinion among my community is a sign of the bounty of Allah."

DAYA (to SITTAH). That's very good!

SALADIN. Continue.

NATHAN. Now back to the rings! The sons sued. And each one swore before the judge that he received the ring from his father's hand. Which was the truth! Each one swore he'd been promised all along that he was to

enjoy the privileges of the ring. Also true! There is no
way his father could have made false promises to him,
each one protested. And rather than cast suspicion on
such a loving father, he'd have to accuse his brothers of
wrongdoing, how ever much he may have trusted them
before. He'd find the traitor out! No question. And he
would take revenge. Even if it meant a thousand years of
war!

DAYA *(to SITTAH)*. Did you hear that? War!

SALADIN. What did the judge say?

NATHAN. He said: "If you can't produce your father right
here and now, I'll have to turn you away. Do you think
I'm here to solve riddles? Or are you waiting for the true
ring to open its mouth?"

HERAKLIOS. This is ridiculous!

SALADIN. Why?

HERAKLIOS. Because in the real world, three rings could
never be so similar!

SITTAH. I have to say, he's absolutely right. Opals? Especially opals. No two are alike.

HERAKLIOS. I call upon the real world! And thus do I re-
fute you!

*(Enter AL-HAFI.)*

NATHAN. Al-Hafi! *(NATHAN is overjoyed to see him,
rushes up to him and embraces him. AL-HAFI slips him
the gold purse NATHAN showed him when he met him
at the caravan.)*

AL-HAFI *(whispering to NATHAN)*. It's all there.

SALADIN. Order! Nathan, we are conducting a trial!

NATHAN. Forgive me. My emotions on seeing my old friend got the better of me. *(Beat.)* Here is the real world. *(NATHAN opens the purse and presents SALADIN's ring, with its tassel. He crosses to SALADIN and SITTAH and shows it to them.)* Here is a real ring of great value. Do you recognize it, O Saladin?

SALADIN. This is the ring of the Ayyubites! Assad's ring! Are you a sorcerer?

NATHAN. You have no idea how I would appreciate it if we could stick to the pending charges for the time being.

SITTAH. Let me see that. *(Examining the ring.)* This is our ring!

NATHAN. Of course it is. See the complex knotted tassel in silk! Only two people in the world know how to tie and read that tassel.

SITTAH. Yes. I'm afraid only two.

NATHAN. Now, look at these two rings, which I have brought back from a market at Samarkand and a Babylonian tomb. *(From the purse NATHAN produces two more rings and presents them to SITTAH.)* They have no knots. But otherwise—?

*(SITTAH examines the three rings, with SALADIN looking on. She holds them up to the light and frowns.)*

SITTAH. These three rings are identical. Each opal shines alike.

SALADIN. Then, using an acceptable endeavor of the mind, Nathan has answered the question Heraklios had a right to ask.

HERAKLIOS. With a parable! That's unacceptably...artistic!

NATHAN. Heraklios, if this friar here used a parable, would that be acceptable?

HERAKLIOS. No.

NATHAN. If the Pope used a parable, would that be acceptable?

HERAKLIOS. No.

NATHAN *(sweetly).* Is there anyone of any stature in your religion who uses parables? *(Pause.)*

SITTAH. I'm pained to say this is unacceptable! Because you and I, brother, know that this is the true ring! We know that! We're sure of it. We're—

HERAKLIOS. Certain!

SALADIN. Certainty is murder.

SITTAH. It's our birthright.

HERAKLIOS. Yes! And on that rock, certainty, Nathan and his pretty fable founder. Everyone knows that Saladin has the real ring! Look! It's tagged!

SITTAH. Why were we so surprised? When Nathan produced the ring? Because we know this is the real ring. The primary ring. The ring of the beloved Ayyubites!

HERAKLIOS. Your parable shatters on the rock of revealed religion.

SALADIN. How do you answer this, Nathan? We know this is our ring. I cannot deny this, even if I wanted to.

NATHAN. I am at my wits' end. I can no more. I lose my life on the same day I lose my daughter. Saladin, I have no more arguments. But I will tell you how an utterly crushed man can submit to God's will and wrest a good deed from horror. *(To BONFILIO.)* You met me with the child at Darun. What you, Bonfilio, don't know *(looks at RECHA)* is that a few days earlier the Christians had murdered all the Jews in Gath, with wives and children.

Among them was my Ruth, my wife, my life, with our seven promising sons. They fled for safety into my brother's house. And there they all were burnt to death.

BONFILIO. Almighty God!

NATHAN. When you, Bonfilio, appeared with the baby Recha, I'd just emerged from dust and ashes. Three days, three nights. Prostrate before God. And weeping! Weeping, did I say? I also argued with Him! I raved and howled and cursed the world and myself. I tell you, man, I swore unending hatred to Christianity!

HERAKLIOS. There! That's it! Burn him!

SALADIN *(icily)*. Oh no. In courts all over the world, hatred is perfectly legal.

DAYA. Oh, yes. In Europe it is the revered basis of our adverbial legal system. *(AL-HAFI signals that DAYA should be still.)* I know, I know. I must mutton my lip.

NATHAN. But reason reasserted itself. Her soft voice told me: "And yet, God is! This also was God's will! Now go! And practice what you've long understood. Surely, it is not harder to practice your belief than to understand it, if you want to. Get up, Nathan!" *(Near tears.)* This was a voice, you see. I stood! I called to God: "I want to! If it is Your will that I should want to!" That moment you, Friar, dismounted and handed me the child, wrapped in your coat. Was she not in your coat, good fellow!

BONFILIO. Aye.

NATHAN. You told me the babe was from my friend, his wife dead, he on the way to battle. I took the child, made it a bed, kissed the babe, fell on my knees and sobbed: "God! For seven, I've got one back already!"

BONFILIO. Nathan! Nathan! You are a Christian! There never was a better Christian!

NATHAN. May you be right! Because what makes me look Christian in your eyes, makes you, good man, look like a Jew to me! *(DAYA looks at AL-HAFI as the meaning of what NATHAN has said sinks in.)* And though *(looking at RECHA)* this strange young girl was soon to bind me to her with more than seven-bonded love, and though the thought is death to me that I should lose my lost sons' love in her again—if Providence wants to reclaim her, I, Nathan, will obey!

HERAKLIOS. The law is a serene goddess, and cares not whether Nathan lost one child or seven.

SITTAH. Furthermore, Recha, you are Wolf von Filnek's daughter, not Nathan's.

*(NATHAN looks at RECHA, who summons her courage: "I'll show you whose daughter I am.")*

RECHA. The true ring has the power to make its owner loved by God and humankind. The imitation rings won't be able to do that. *(RECHA suddenly turns on NATHAN, HERAKLIOS, SITTAH and SALADIN.)* Well? Are you? Loved by God and humankind? You People of the Book? Well, are you? I know you love yourselves, but which of you is loved by the other two? That is something I'd really like to know. Because, down through the ages and no doubt into ages to come, you're always at war! Why, are any of you loved by the others? You love yourself alone and don't care about the others! Isn't that what this war is about? And all the many wars to come? Why, there's only one man in this room who is loved by Christian, Muslim and Jew, and you're trying to kill him!

DAYA *(confidentially to SITTAH)*. Nathan and I brought her up very well.

CURD. And what about the future? We're in a magic bubble of time. Truce in Jerusalem! I challenge the three religions to prove by their actions that they have the true ring!

SALADIN. I'd like to take up your challenge, Templar. But I know I have the true ring. And certainty is murder.

HERAKLIOS. It's hopeless, don't you see? Saladin knows he has the true ring. He can't escape that inheritance. Nor can I. We are condemned to be certain.

SITTAH. It's the tassel, you see.

CURD. Well, then, if it's the tassel that makes us sure, cut it off!

SALADIN. I can't give up Assad's ring. Not to anyone.

NATHAN *(holding up the prayer book)*. Not even to its owner? Friar Bonfilio, what is this?

BONFILIO. That's Wolf von Filnek's prayer book. I took it from his body when at Askalon I buried him. *(BONFILIO makes the sign of the cross and rubs his hands together.)* So help me God. *(BONFILIO sees blood appear on his palms. No one else sees it.)* And now I've given all any mortal can. May I leave? I promised to help the sick at Siloa.

SALADIN. You may.

HERAKLIOS. With my blessing.

*(BONFILIO approaches HERAKLIOS, stumbles, and steadies himself by grasping HERAKLIOS' garment. As he does so, he leaves a smear of blood on HERAKLIOS' sleeve. HERAKLIOS is unaware of it. HERAKLIOS*

*blesses him, and BONFILIO exits without a trace of his
former subservience.)*

NATHAN. Behold this book. Saladin. Von Filnek writes in
   Arabic script, and is, like you, a Kurd. He describes his
   family. Here. *(NATHAN hands the prayer book to
   SALADIN. SALADIN reads it. He looks at NATHAN.
   NATHAN returns the look coolly.)*
HERAKLIOS *(pointing to the book)*. What possible rele-
   vance! A dead man's relic! *(HERAKLIOS sees the blood
   on his sleeve, murmurs to himself.)* Blood. *(HERAKLIOS
   looks at the stains in wonder, and then stares at the
   doorway through which BONFILIO disappeared.)*
SITTAH *(turning her attention to HERAKLIOS)*. Are you
   well?
HERAKLIOS. Leave me alone.
SALADIN. Sittah. Sittah, look at this.
SITTAH *(crosses to SALADIN)*. All the names of our fam-
   ily. Written by Assad! He took the name von Filnek.
SALADIN *(to RECHA)*. You are Assad's daughter.
SITTAH. The daughter of Assad! The line of the
   Ayyubites lives!
SALADIN *(to all)*. The Templar's mother was Maria von
   Stauffen. *(To CURD.)* To protect you in wartime, she
   gave you to her brother, Conrad, a Templar, who raised
   you and gave you his name. Curd is short for Conrad.
CURD. Why is my mother in the prayer book of Assad?
AL-HAFI *(to DAYA)*. Why do I think I know the answer to
   this?
DAYA *(to AL-HAFI)*. Oh, Al-Hafi! This is irretrievable!
SITTAH. Why shouldn't she be? Maria von Stauffen was
   Assad's wife.

*(CURD and RECHA look at each other.)*

CURD *(to RECHA)*. Sister?
RECHA. So it would appear.
CURD *(approaching RECHA)*. I am so…relieved!
RECHA. And so am I! You have no idea.
CURD. Yes, I do.
RECHA. No, you don't.
CURD. I do.
RECHA. You don't!
CURD. I'm in the same boat, sister!
RECHA. No, you're not!
CURD. I am!
RECHA. I give. You are. We are.
CURD. Recha! Dear, bold, adorable sister! *(Beat; finally smiles.)* You'll find me much more adept *(gives her a friendly slug)* at this new kind of love!
RECHA. Dear, daring, hotheaded, handsome brother! That's why my knees were so strong! *(She returns the friendly slug.)*
DAYA *(scandalized)*. Oh, my! *(To AL-HAFI.)* Soon there's not going to be any distance left between anyone in the world. What are we going to do?

*(HERAKLIOS is looking at the blood on his surplice.)*

CURD. Improve the world. Saladin. I am the son of Assad. *(CURD takes the tasseled ring from SITTAH and holds it up.)* This is my ring. Will you remove the tassel with your scimitar?
SALADIN. I shall. With my scimitar.

*(SALADIN takes his scimitar. With a lightning riff of his blade, SALADIN cuts the tassel off, never touching the ring. MUSIC sting. SITTAH takes the ring. She takes the other two rings and holds them. Then she gives all three rings to SALADIN, HERAKLIOS and NATHAN. They look at the rings and hold them up to the light.)*

SALADIN *(cont'd)*. No one can tell which is the true ring. It may well be that all three are. The Koran says—

DAYA *(beaming at AL-HAFI)*. I am very interested to hear this. What *does* the Koran say?

SALADIN. God has sent messengers to every people on the face of the earth.

DAYA. Oh! To Jerusalem as well as France. Then we are one.

SALADIN. Therefore, with the certainty gone, we must strive in offices of love. *(To HERAKLIOS and NATHAN.)* In which you will find me an ally.

HERAKLIOS. I am content.

AL-HAFI. Amen to that say I!

DAYA *(taking AL-HAFI's hand)*. And most furtively amen.

AL-HAFI. Beauteous Daya, will you run off with me to India or to Anjou? Will you help me to strive in offices of love?

DAYA. Yes, my dervish darling! We'll run to every land that has had a prophet! And wherever we run, I'll give you all the strife you could ever wish for! I'm your grape!

SALADIN. A thousand years from now, let a just judge decide if the people of Islam, the Jews, or the Christians are—

HERAKLIOS. —because of their deeds—

NATHAN. —not their claims—

SALADIN. —loved by humankind and by God.

**END**

# GLOSSARY

| | |
|---|---|
| Ayyubites | dynasty founded by Saladin |
| Hadith | maxims of the prophet Muhammad |
| Hajj | Muslim pilgrimage to Mecca |
| Ijtihad | independent reasoning |
| Shahadah | Muslim proclamation of faith |
| Shariah | Islamic holy law |
| Sunnah | customs imitating the actions of the prophet Muhammad |
| Zakat | alms given to assist the poor |

# DIRECTOR'S NOTES

# DIRECTOR'S NOTES